THE LEGEND OF AMP

"F" Crimp for Open Barrel Terminals

The AMP Heritage Room displays decades of history. The Heritage Room, located in the Global Executive Leadership Center, was opened to employees and the public in November, 1996.

THE LEGEND OF
AMP

JEFFREY L. RODENGEN

Also by Jeff Rodengen

The Legend of Chris-Craft

IRON FIST: *The Lives of Carl Kiekhaefer*

Evinrude-Johnson and The Legend of OMC

Serving The Silent Service: The Legend of Electric Boat

The Legend of Dr Pepper/Seven-Up

The Legend of Honeywell

The Legend of Briggs & Stratton

The Legend of Ingersoll-Rand

The Legend of Stanley: 150 Years of The Stanley Works

The MicroAge Way

The Legend of Halliburton

The Legend of York International

The Legend of Nucor Corporation

The Legend of Goodyear: The First 100 Years

The Legend of Cessna

The Legend of Echlin

The Legend of AMD

The Legend of Amdahl

Applied Materials: Pioneering the Information Age

The Legend of Pfizer

Publisher's Cataloging in Publication
Prepared by Quality Books Inc.

Rodengen, Jeffrey L.
    The legend of AMP /Jeffrey L. Rodengen.
    p. cm.
    Includes bibliographical references and index.
    ISBN 0-945903-33-2

    1. AMP Incorporated 2. Electronic industries—United States.
I. Title

    HD9696.U6R64 1997   338.7'621381'0973
                                   QBI97-40433

Write Stuff Enterprises, Inc.

1515 Southeast 4th Avenue • Fort Lauderdale, FL 33316
1-800-900-Book (1-800-900-2665) • (954) 462-6657

Library of Congress Catalog Card Number 96-61251
ISBN 0-945903-33-2

Completely produced in the United States of America
10 9 8 7 6 5 4 3 2 1

TABLE OF CONTENTS

INTRODUCTION

A T 41 YEARS OF age, Uncas Aeneas Whitaker was a successful engineer with a secure job. But he wasn't satisfied, and by 1941 he was searching for something to challenge his entrepreneurial spirit.

Whitaker discovered his opportunity in Stephen Buchanan, founder of Industrial Manufacturers. Buchanan, something of an odd tinkerer, had patented a solderless electrical terminal and started the small New Jersey-based company to sell his products. Whitaker immediately saw the potential in these innovative terminal devices and struck an agreement with Buchanan. On September 15, 1941, Aero-Marine Products, Inc., was born with U.A. Whitaker as vice president and treasurer.

The world was ready for the revolutionary solderless terminal. In 1941, America was on the eve of war and the military was looking for ways to build strong, light aircraft. Until A-MP's innovative terminals were introduced, electrical connections had primarily relied on soldering, which required flux, heat and skill to master. By contrast, a solderless terminal could be easily slid onto the end of a wire and crimped in place with a special tool. The terminals caught on immediately and at the end of its second year in business, A-MP had amassed a $500,000 backlog in orders.

From its earliest days of selling terminals to aircraft manufacturers, AMP has worked on a simple principle: Discover what the customer needs and supply it.

AMP was positioned on the leading edge of a boom in electrical and electronic devices. And each innovation, from the modernization and proliferation of household appliances to the earliest transistorized calculators, required new methods of electrical connection. AMP engineers had to teach customers that their new designs would save money, last longer and result in a better connection.

Within a decade, AMP's product catalog offered thousands of specialized connection devices. Within the development labs at the Harrisburg, Pennsylvania, headquarters, inventors were allowed to transform new ideas into products. Whitaker, himself an engineer, focused attention on quality and applied cost, instead of price per unit. The company's official slogan was, "Precision Engineering at the end of Wire." But Whitaker informally urged his engineers to take the simple electrical connection device and "engineer the hell out of it." Some famous early AMP products include the Standard B terminal and the Pre-Insulated Diamond Grip terminal.

After World War II, consumer demand boomed. Television antennae sprouted from rooftops, and households snapped up labor-saving devices such as washing machines and dishwashers. On the highways, drivers celebrated the country's prosperity by demanding larger and more complex cars. And in the office, a company called IBM was moving into the high-tech world of computers. AMP was there at every turn and before long, the company was the world's leading supplier of electrical connection devices and the automatic machines used to apply them.

By 1960, the increasingly technical demands of electronic products were pushing manufacturers in a new direction: connectors. When AMP introduced the M-Series connector (named M for its military origins), the company signalled that it was ready to become a powerful supplier to this emerging industry. Over the next few years, successful products followed one after another: the AMPMODU interconnection system, the PICABOND telephone cable connection system, and in the 1970s, the AMPLIMITE, and AMP-LATCH, and CHAMP families of connectors.

AMP was already playing in a global arena. AMP had followed IBM to France in the early 1950s. After sensing the incredible potential overseas, other facilities soon followed: Great Britain, Holland, Japan, Italy, Australia, Canada and Puerto Rico. New products introduced in Harrisburg quickly circulated around the world, driven by AMP's superior design and aggressive marketing.

Whitaker died in 1975, the year the company headed into a recession-induced sales slump. The heady electronics boom temporarily slowed and manufacturers became overstocked. Orders suddenly ceased. Despite the severity of the recession and "stagflation" throughout these hard years, AMP's earlier policies paid off. The company had expanded its narrow product line of electrical connection devices into a wide spectrum of strategic industries, and within so many countries, that sales exceeded $1 billion in 1979.

In the 1980s, a second wave of innovation swept the manufacturing industry, this one provoked by miniaturization and ever more demanding competition. Over the course of the decade, AMP moved into supplying complete subassemblies and began to retool its manufacturing processes to comply with concepts like Total Quality Management, Value Added manufacturing and product, and Ship to Stock.

Then in 1985, the electronics industry underwent the most significant correction in its short history, and AMP was brought face to face with what would be its biggest challenge: the sudden and rapid globalization of industry. AMP's customers had become multinational corporations, as had AMP. These customers wanted the same product, service and price in Singapore that they had in Kansas. In the late 1980s, AMP began to look at its international operations and see "dukedoms" instead of a seamless business unit. When Bill Hudson, CEO and president, and Jim Marley, chairman, took over in 1993, they made it their first priority to accelerate the change in the way that AMP did business around the world. They announced the Vision 2000 goals, including accelerating the growth rate of the company, and committed AMP to a three-part basic strategy of maintaining leadership in the connection device industry, diversifying into related product and market areas, and expanding into new global markets.

Into the next millennium, this is the principal challenge that AMP is facing. The company is organizing itself into market-oriented business units that recognize no boundaries, while remaining geographically responsive. AMP's business model organizes the company in a matrix that encompasses regional focus, industry-specific business units and the company's technological core competencies.

Through the expansion of its business units and the careful acquisition of new technologies, AMP has tripled the size of the markets it now addresses. AMP has become a quiet but pervasive presence in every day life. Walk into any average home and AMP products are behind the walls, in the telephones, the televisions, the computers and the appliances. AMP products conduct and route the electricity that turns on our headlights and stops our cars.

Whitaker founded his company with a simple belief in his people and the never-ending pursuit of quality. He recruited strong people who made the company grow by skillfully pursuing the myriad of opportunities arising from economic growth and technological change. All of AMP's subsequent chairmen and CEOs joined AMP when Whitaker was still CEO: the leadership torch passed smoothly from Whitaker to Sam Auchincloss and George Ingalls in the 1960s, to Joe Brenner and Cleve Fredricksen in the 1970s, to Walter Raab in the 1980s, to Hal McInnes in 1990, and to Bill Hudson and Jim Marley in 1993.

Now more than 50 years later, Hudson and Marley have reaffirmed the same basic principles that made AMP successful, while reshaping the company to compete in a vastly changed business environment. As the world continues to change and AMP continues to transform itself, the company will move ever closer toward its goal of $10 billion in sales.

AMP has come a long way. By 1997, AMP had grown to a worldwide organization of more than 45,000 people in 244 facilities in 50 countries with sales approaching $6 billion and 20 percent of its business diversified into cables, cable assemblies, printed circuit boards, panel assemblies, electro-optic devices, sensors, touch screen data entry systems, and networking products. A very solid foundation has been laid for continued long-term growth.

ACKNOWLEDGMENTS

Researching, writing and publishing *The Legend of AMP* would not have been possible without the assistance and cooperation of many people.

The development of the historical timelines and the archival research was accomplished by my hard-working and resourceful research assistant Jon Rounds. His careful and thorough research made it possible to publish much new and fascinating information about the origins of this truly innovative organization.

The candid insights of AMP executives were of particular importance to the project. I am especially grateful to CEO and President William J. Hudson, Chairman James E. Marley, and Corporate Vice President and Chief Financial Officer Robert Ripp.

Sel Friedlander, who retired in January 1997 as director of corporate staff services and staff assistant to Chairman Jim Marley, was instrumental in providing information and many interviews with long-time AMP employees and retirees.

I am also grateful to the host of executives, current and retired, whose experiences helped shape the company: Harold A. McInnes, retired in 1993 as president, chairman and CEO; Walter F. Raab, retired in 1990 as chairman and CEO; Joseph D. Brenner, retired in 1982 as president, chairman and CEO; Herbert M. Cole, corporate vice president and president, AMP Asia/Pacific; John Gurski, corporate vice president and president, AMP Global Operations Division; Ted Dalrymple, corporate vice president, Global Marketing; Charles W. Goonrey, corporate vice president and general legal counsel; Philip G. Guarneschelli, corporate vice president and chief Human Resource officer; David Henschel, corpo-

rate secretary; Joseph C. Overbaugh, corporate treasurer; William S. Urkiel, corporate controller; and Phillipe LeMaitre, corporate vice president and chief technology officer.

AMP's divisional vice presidents and other executives, both past and present, provided interesting insights and anecdotes: Peter Glaser, Global Manufacturing; Juergen W. Gromer, president, AMP Global Automotive Division; Leonard I. Hill, Jr., Global Succession & Organization Planning; Dean R. Hooper, Jr., Global Customer Satisfaction & Business Effectiveness; John H. Kegel, Logistics, Supplier Relations, ASG; G. Russell Knerr, Jr., AMP Building Systems, GISB, who retired in 1997; Linn Lightner, Global Engineering Assurance; Howard R. Peiffer, Global Technology; Nazario Proietto, president, AMP Global Power and Utilities Division; Carol A. Ritter; Global Power and Utilities, Americas; J.C. Tan, Asia/Pacific — South; H. Chester Timmins, retired in 1997 as regional business executive, Motor Vehicles, the Americas; Ronald F. Vance, Chief Information Officer; and Merrill A. Yohe, Jr., Public Affairs; Bill Narigan, retired vice president of quality; David Toser, regional controller; Bill Oakland, former director of Investor Relations; Henry Line, vice president, Global Standards; Bill Broske, former research associate; Daniel Burnand, former sales and marketing manager for AMP de France; Wilson "Ben" Connor, former corporate vice president, director of Marketing; Dominique Chauvin, former general manager of AMP de France and AMP Brazil; David Crockett, former marketing director in the International Division; Al Curtis, former advertising manager; Walter "Gordon" Drane, former director of Special

Communication Projects; Rudy Eckhardt, area director of Eastern Europe; Tom Freedom, former manager of environmental testing; Franz Gall, former general sales manager for Benelux, Scandinavia and Switzerland; Jean Gorjat, retired in 1995 as corporate vice president of AMP Asia/Pacific; Alfred Greger, retired in 1994 as general manager in Switzerland and Austria; Harry Kennis, general sales manager of Benelux countries; Homer Henschen, retired director, Advanced Manufacturing Technologies; William Lange, retired corporate vice president and director of Merchandising; Joe Maher, vice president, Marketing and Sales Planning; Ken Neijstrom, former vice president, General Products; Dennis Morse, retired in 1990 as managing director of AMP Great Britain Limited; Bob Nishiyama, retired in 1985 as general manager, AMP Japan; S. Wilson Pollock, retired in 1980 as corporate vice president of Engineering and Research; Vittorio Pozzi, director product marketing southern Europe; Stuart Prince, retired in 1991 as management of International Patent and Legal Department; Jay L. Seitchik, president of the Whitaker Corp.; Richard Skaare, director Corporate Communications; Robert Suares, general manager of the AMP Export Company; Joe Sweeney, retired vice president of Technology; George Tsygalnitzky, retired in 1974 as general sales manager and director of export in London; Leon Whipple, former director and staff analyst for U.A. Whitaker; and Dottie Yingling, former manager, Business Analysis; Dimitry Grabbe, AMP Fellow; John Hopkins, retired corporate vice president; Marshall Holcombe, retired chief patent attorney; and Don Shoemaker, retired vice president of the Connector and Component Group.

AMP employees who helped with information gathering and photographs include Kathy Cohn, administrative assistant; Edward Hirshman, product manager, Automachine Systems Group; Thea Hocker, manager, Public Relations; Nadine Rockovich, former Public Affairs assistant; Mary Rakoczy, manager, Shareholder Services; Kathy Shader, administrative assistant, photography; George Wallace, Jr., supervisor, photography; and Ted Webber, marketing communication.

Finally, a very special word of thanks to the staff at Write Stuff Enterprises, Inc.: Executive Editor Alex Lieber, Associate Editor Jon VanZile, Creative Director Kyle Newton, Art Directors Sandy Cruz and Jill Apolinario, Production Manager Fred Moll, Marketing and Sales Manager Christopher J. Frosch, Bookkeeper and Office Manager Marianne Roberts, Logistics Specialist Rafael Santiago, Executive Assistant Jill Thomas and Project Coordinator Karine N. Rodengen.

The company U.A. Whitaker would transform into AMP, Incorporated, found its humble origins within this Elizabeth, New Jersey, building in 1941.

CHAPTER ONE

U.A. WHITAKER AND THE FOUNDING OF AMP

1900–1941

"I have become, during the course of my investigation, so thoroughly interested in the possibilities of the proposition that, granting suitable and adequate arrangements can be made, I am willing to divorce myself gradually from my present highly satisfactory connection and devote eventually my full time, energy and capacity towards its full development."

— U.A. Whitaker[1]

UNCAS AENEAS WHITAKER did not fit the profile of a typical risk-taker. At 41 years old, he was an accomplished engineer with dozens of patents to his name, a steady job with a big company and three college degrees. Nevertheless, he spent the summer of 1941 considering a tremendous risk that could jeopardize his income and future. To those who didn't know him, it would have appeared out of character — Whitaker's business habits tended toward the methodical, his physical appearance was stern and dour. But in his chest beat the heart of an entrepreneur with a flair for engineering and managing people.

Whitaker was studying a business opportunity with a small New Jersey manufacturing company. The operation produced an inexpensive and simple product: a two-cent terminal that could be crimped onto the end of a wire. Most terminals at the time were soldered, which left room for human error and required expertise and special materials. Crimped terminals, on the other hand, appeared to offer convenience, speed and durability.

Whitaker was intrigued by both the product and the company. Writing to his father, he said one of the main reasons the deal appealed to him was that it would give him the chance to become "a big part of a small company rather than a small part of a big company."[2]

Whitaker also saw potential in the tiny, stamped pieces of metal. This was the summer after Nazi Germany had overrun most of Europe and the Japanese had taken control over huge areas of China. Dark war clouds inched ever closer to home. As Whitaker studied his options, the U.S. economy began gearing up for serious wartime production, with record numbers of airplanes rolling off assembly lines all over the country. Every one of those aircraft would need multitudes of lightweight and strong electrical connections. The solderless terminal was perfect and Whitaker knew it.

The Formative Years

Uncas Aeneas Whitaker was born in Lincoln, Kansas, on March 22, 1900, the third of four children, to Oliver Barr (O.B.) and Annetta Ruth Whitaker. His rare blend of Midwestern work ethic, skill, entrepreneurial zeal and conservative politics was surely a reflection of the values taught to him by his father.

Aircraft-Marine's original success was due to the simple idea that a terminal could be slid onto the end of a wire and crimped in place.

O.B. Whitaker (1869-1942) was a man of many talents. He began his career as an educator who had earned five college degrees, and went on to become a Missouri state legislator, bank president, novelist and farm real estate speculator. His favorite author was James Fenimore Cooper, and he named his third-born child after Uncas, the noble Indian chief portrayed as the title character in *The Last of the Mohicans*.[3]

In 1913, the Whitaker family moved from Kansas to Weaubleau, Missouri. Uncas was sent to high school at the Drury Academy, 50 miles away in Springfield. In 1918, he attended Drury College before transferring the next year to the Missouri School of Mines and Metallurgy in Rolla, where he excelled in electrical engineering, mechanics and machine shop, earning an overall average of B plus.[4]

In the fall of 1920, Uncas again transferred, this time to the Massachusetts Institute of Technology. The jump from small Midwestern college to premiere engineering school proved too challenging. In 1922, Whitaker flunked three courses: Applied Mechanics, Heat Engineering and Materials of Engineering. However, school policy allowed students to retake final exams in failed courses, and Whitaker successfully passed all three the next year. He earned his first degree, a bachelor of science in mechanical engineering, in 1923.[5]

After graduation, Whitaker took his first job with Westinghouse Air Brake in Pittsburgh, Pennsylvania. George Westinghouse had engineered the railroad air brake, gradually developing it into a reliable device by the late 1800s, and his company continued to perfect the technology and patent new developments. Westinghouse engineers were given great freedom to invent and create. As Whitaker biographer William Cohn explained, "To let the talented engineer make his own successes and suffer his own failures was a philosophy Whitaker would apply to his own engineering department some years later."[6]

Whitaker thrived in this new environment of applied technology, where engineers were given the freedom to develop and refine their designs. During his time at Westinghouse, he was credited with 52 patents, of which 22 were domestic and 30 were foreign.

In June 1929, Whitaker earned a degree in electrical engineering from the Carnegie Institute of Technology (now Carnegie-Mellon), where he

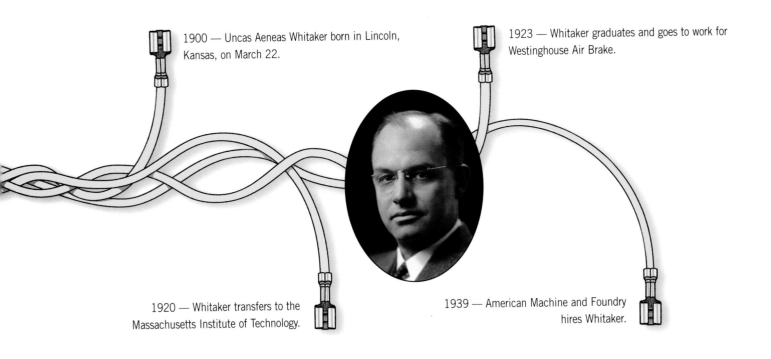

1900 — Uncas Aeneas Whitaker born in Lincoln, Kansas, on March 22.

1923 — Whitaker graduates and goes to work for Westinghouse Air Brake.

1920 — Whitaker transfers to the Massachusetts Institute of Technology.

1939 — American Machine and Foundry hires Whitaker.

Whitaker's first job was with George Westinghouse at Westinghouse Air Brake. Shown with the apprentice class of 1923, he is at the far left on the bottom row. Others include: (top row, left to right) A.S. Benton, V.D. Bethge, S.L Williams, H.I. Detro; (second row, left to right) C.R. Guthrie, H.J. Watson, G.L. Cotter, H.M. Potter; (front, left to right) Whitaker, G.M. McWilliams, N.T. Mann, C.S. Davis and Westinghouse.

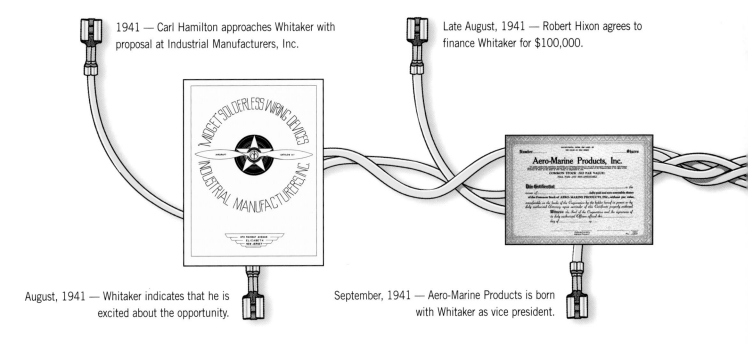

1941 — Carl Hamilton approaches Whitaker with proposal at Industrial Manufacturers, Inc.

Late August, 1941 — Robert Hixon agrees to finance Whitaker for $100,000.

August, 1941 — Whitaker indicates that he is excited about the opportunity.

September, 1941 — Aero-Marine Products is born with Whitaker as vice president.

Pictured in the 1940s, Whitaker already was an accomplished engineer with three college degrees and a solid career behind him.

had enrolled for advanced studies. Shortly after graduation, he left Westinghouse to join the Hoover Company in North Canton, Ohio, where he was named director of Development and Design. During his nine years with the company, he contributed many patents for design improvements to vacuum cleaners. More importantly, he discovered what he believed was the key to Hoover's success: superior engineering. Despite its reliance on a single product during the Depression years, the company thrived because its product was simply /better engineered than competing products.[7] During his time at Hoover, Whitaker studied law, earning a degree from Cleveland Law School in 1935.

In January 1939, Whitaker was hired away from Hoover by American Machine and Foundry, a New York-based firm that manufactured equipment for sewing machines and bakeries as well as the tobacco industry. American Machine and Foundry named him director of Research and Standards and charged him with reorganizing the company's plants and manufacturing processes. He was heavily involved with machine design, cost analysis and patents.[8]

Throughout Whitaker's early career, he made strong impressions on the engineers and executives with whom he associated, many of whom would later figure prominently in the growth and leadership of his own company. At Westinghouse Air Brake, he met Frank Wells, later to become Whitaker's first director of research; at Hoover, he met Vern Carlson, later his first chief engineer at A-MP; at American Machine and Foundry, he met head accountant George Ingalls, who became a lifelong friend, financial advisor and eventually president of AMP.

Leon Whipple, who worked for Whitaker at American Machine and Foundry and began a long career at A-MP in 1955, was struck by Whitaker's concern for employees:

> *"I first met U.A. Whitaker in 1940. He was building a staff of young engineers for the engineering department of American Machine and Foundry in Brooklyn. For the next 35 years the characteristic that most impressed me was his deep interest and concern for his employees.*
>
> *"Most of the young engineers were from small towns in the Midwest. To build a team spirit, Mr. Whitaker and his two assistants, Frank Wells and F. 'Len' Pierce, organized a monthly dinner and card party for the staff. A group dinner at a Manhattan restaurant was followed by an evening of cards, also in Manhattan. We were all able to talk with the three staff leaders on an informal basis. I believe Mr. Whitaker was genuinely interested in getting to know his staff."[9]*

Getting Started

In 1940, the Chicago-based management consultant firm of Booz, Fry, Allen and Hamilton was searching for an executive to fill a top position at a small vacuum cleaner firm. By this time, Whitaker had established himself as a superior engineer and manager, so Edwin Booz contacted him about the position.

Whitaker, ready for something new, carefully studied the offer but declined.

Both Booz and one of his partners, Carl Hamilton, were deeply impressed with Whitaker. In a 1997 interview, Hamilton's grandson, William Lane III, said, "My grandfather did have the sense that the guy in front of him was a genius."[10] When they asked what kind of situation would interest him, Whitaker replied that it would have to be "a long-term connection that he could build into something big," preferably a company that had a product with potential for development and could attract financial backing.[11]

Hamilton introduced Whitaker to F.C. "Colonel" Hixon, who was president and portfolio manager of Midland Investment Company. Hixon also recognized Whitaker's potential, and a search began to find a suitable opportunity. The search led to Stephen Buchanan, owner of Industrial Manufacturers, Inc., a small manufacturing firm based in Elizabeth, New Jersey. Buchanan had founded his company with two investors, Trigve Skyberg and Charles Shoemaker. But the association had proven unsatisfactory. Skyberg and Shoemaker, after providing an initial modest investment to launch the company, did little more than financial paperwork.[12] Thus it happened that Buchanan in 1941 was looking for new business partners.

Carl Hamilton turned out to be, in the words of corporate historian Bern Sharfman, the "midwife to the birth of this new company."[13] He arranged for a meeting between Whitaker and Buchanan in June 1941. Whitaker came away from the meeting intrigued with Industrial Manufacturers' main product, the solderless terminal. But typical of his methodical approach to any venture, Whitaker undertook an intensive study of Buchanan, the product and the company before making a decision.

Stephen Buchanan and Industrial Manufacturers, Inc.

In a 28-page report to Hamilton, dated August 12, 1941, Whitaker presented his findings on Industrial Manufacturers, Inc., and Buchanan: "I find him to be an interesting, cooperative and inventive type of individual with a very creditable record of accomplishment in his prior connections. [He] was born in the Carolinas. He had no formal education beyond high school. He received his technical training by working for various electrical firms."[14]

Between 1916 and 1919, Buchanan had worked as a master electrician for the Baltimore Dry Dock Company, responsible for maintaining and repairing electrical equipment on U.S. and British Navy ships. In 1925, after a stint as an electrical contractor, he became a development and sales engineer for Thomas & Betts, an Elizabeth, New Jersey-based electrical parts firm.

During his 15 years at Thomas & Betts, Buchanan claimed he had "contributed 90 percent of the ideas upon which the company's solderless terminals business was built, all of which played an important part in enabling Thomas & Betts Company to expand their business from the vol-

An Industrial Manufacturers, Inc., early catalog offered two main products: solderless terminals and bonding jumpers for aircraft manufacture.

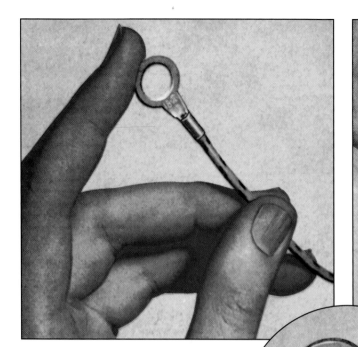

ume of $600,000 to approximately $6,000,000 over this period."[15]

Whitaker's search of the United States Patent Office confirmed Buchanan's claim. Thirty patents were indeed issued in Buchanan's name between 1927 and 1939. Also, Whitaker's professional inquiries substantiated Buchanan's claim that he "probably did contribute the vast majority of the patentable ideas" on which Thomas & Betts' solderless terminal business was built.[16]

Buchanan left Thomas & Betts in 1939, when he was in his mid-fifties, to found Industrial Manufacturers and hopefully make more money. He remained in Elizabeth, setting up an office in a converted house on Rahway Avenue and a production facility in the Bayway Terminal Building.[17]

The new company's product line was limited to two basic items: solderless terminals and bonding jumpers. Bonding jumpers were "used to bond electrically various parts of an airplane so as to prevent radio noises caused by static electricity passing from one part of the ship to another."[18] Two-thirds of the company's business was terminals and splices, and Whitaker estimated

that 98 percent of all sales were military-related.

Since Buchanan's original patents were owned by Thomas & Betts, Buchanan modified his inventions and obtained new patents for the slightly different terminals and jumpers.

Industrial Manufacturers, Inc., did "very little actual manufacturing" internally. Whitaker's inventory of equipment listed only 15 pieces, including "eight Stimpson foot-operated riveters or punch presses" and some standard shop equipment, including a "portable electric drill and stand" and a bench grinder. "Copper and aluminum tubing is purchased, cut to length and is then strung on cable and put through two power punch press operations, inspected and packed on the company's premises."[19]

Applying solderless terminals was easy and fast. Insulation is stripped off and the wire slips easily into the serrated terminal barrel (above left). Unskilled workers can perform uniform crimping operations with the hand crimping tool notched for proper wire gauge (above right). When finished, the A-MP solderless terminal is securely applied (inset). The quality of the electrical joint can be determined by visual inspection.

Despite the meager facilities and equipment, the company's products were well-engineered. Whitaker reported that Buchanan's terminals and splices were "the simplest and lightest on the market," met all military specifications, and were in every way "the equal of Thomas & Betts' terminals."[20]

Whitaker concluded that Buchanan "probably knows as much about solderless terminals as anyone in the country. In addition to this, he is creative and has the knack of devising small devices to fit certain exact requirements."[21] Whitaker also found that Buchanan had key ties among military contractors. He was "on exceedingly friendly terms with all these people and seems to have their complete confidence. ... This is evidenced by the fact that the only two solderless electrical terminals which have Navy or War Department approval have been devised and created by him."[22]

It is interesting to note that Whitaker's generous assessment of Buchanan contrasted with others' opinions of the man. Whitaker's own secretary, for one, described Buchanan as "brawny and vulgar."[23] This discrepancy suggests a key ingredient to Whitaker's success as a leader — his tendency to see the positive aspects of a person's character.

Solderless Terminals and Military Aircraft

But ultimately it wasn't because of Buchanan that Whitaker liked what he saw in Industrial Manufacturers, Inc. Instead, he was attracted to the massive potential in Buchanan's simple product during the wartime aircraft and shipbuilding boom.

When World War II began in 1939, the American aircraft industry produced 5,856 planes. One year later, after Germany's air superiority had been frightfully demonstrated over Europe, President Franklin D. Roosevelt ordered production of 50,000 planes per year. This tremendous expansion was achieved, but only through a frantic manufacturing campaign that involved cooperation among all aircraft manufacturers and other industries, including automobile makers. In the end, American industry produced an amazing 300,000 planes between 1940 and 1945.[24]

Naval aircraft at the Matagorda Island Bombing and Gunnery Range in 1943. American industry rose to the challenge presented by the world war. (Photo courtesy of Brown & Root.)

Connections were crucial details of aircraft manufacture. As a wartime article in a trade magazine explained, "An electrical system is as good as its connections. ... [Connection failures] on domestic appliances are not generally serious but on aircraft may involve many lives, much valuable equipment, and, in fact, the success of our war effort."[25]

The accepted method of soldering connections, if done correctly, produced reliable results. Wires were simply soldered together, or a terminal could be soldered to the end of a wire and then screwed to an instrument, terminal block or receiver clip.[26] The connection provided little electrical resistance, and therefore minimal heat buildup, and it resisted corrosion. However, compared to crimping, soldering was a slow process.

It also required a certain amount of skill, and the process itself involved several variables, including heat, flux, solder type and cleanliness of surfaces. Insufficient heat, the wrong flux and dirty surfaces could all affect the reliability of a soldered connection.[27] Also, soldering was awkward in hard-to-reach places such as the tight quarters of an airplane.[28]

Solderless terminals, on the other hand, could be applied six to seven times as fast in the field and twice as fast in the factory.[29] In 1941, though Buchanan and his former company, Thomas &

As the American aircraft industry geared up for war production, A-MP terminals were used by major airframe companies like Lockheed.

The Martin A-26/B-26 Invader was one of the first converts to Aircraft-Marine's innovative new solderless terminal designs.

Betts, had made inroads, the solderless terminal, which sold for only $20 per thousand, was far from being generally accepted by aircraft manufacturers, or for that matter anyone else.

One of the few converts to solderless terminals was the Glenn L. Martin Company of Baltimore, maker of the B-26 middle-range bomber. Founded in 1912, the company was one of the top airframe manufacturers in the country by the outbreak of World War II, and, along with Boeing, Douglas and Lockheed, was recognized as one of the most technologically innovative firms in the nation.[30] In 1940, Martin was awarded a contract to produce 1,000 B-26 bombers. Buchanan's fledgling company became Martin's chief supplier of terminals.[31]

Whitaker was convinced that the Martin contract was the tip of a very large iceberg. Whitaker estimated one large bomber alone required $300 worth of terminals and jumpers. Using these figures, he calculated a potential market of at least $5 million in aircraft products alone.[32]

Whitaker's Conclusions

But Whitaker's enthusiasm for the new venture was not without reservations.

One of his chief concerns was patent protection for Buchanan's products. Although Whitaker's research showed that Buchanan's new patents did not infringe on the similar ones he had developed for Thomas & Betts, Whitaker saw the situation as a double-edged sword: If Buchanan could modify his own designs to avoid infringement, so could anyone, including competitors. Whitaker suggested the new company would have to investigate ways to protect new products through "patent structure."[33]

Whitaker also was disturbed by Industrial Manufacturers' reliance on outside suppliers and manufacturers. It was logical that wartime scarcity of goods and services would drive up prices, and Whitaker predicted the new company would have to develop manufacturing capabilities of its own.[34]

A third potential problem was competitors, who would be attracted to the profits that solderless terminals were generating for both Buchanan and Thomas & Betts. In order to stay ahead of the field, Whitaker recommended a policy of constant research to develop new products and improve existing ones, and of "intimate contact" with the company's major customers to assess and respond to their needs.[35]

Although Whitaker seemed fully aware of the pitfalls inherent in starting a single-product company during a wartime economy, he saw the war as a window of opportunity in which to build "in less time than is ordinarily required" a broader-based company with long-term potential.[36]

In retrospect, Whitaker's assessment of the situation facing Industrial Manufacturers reflected some of the key business philosophies he would use so successfully in later decades: reliance on in-house manufacturing, attention to patents and engineering, investment in research and development, and a close relationship with customers.

Whitaker Launches Aero-Marine Products, Inc.

With problems identified and solutions in hand, Whitaker came into Industrial Manufacturers eager to develop the company into something big. In his report to Carl Hamilton, Whitaker wrote:

"I have become, during the course of my investigation, so thoroughly interested in the possibilities of the proposition that, granting suitable and adequate arrangements can be made, I am willing to divorce myself gradually from my present highly satisfactory connection and devote eventually my full time, energy and capacity towards its full development."[37]

The immediate need was financing. Again, it was Carl Hamilton who found the answer. He once again approached Midland Investment Company, which had offices in the same Chicago building as Booz, Fry, Allen and Hamilton and controlled multimillion-dollar holdings in lumber, gas and oil. The Hixon family was impressed and agreed to commit Midland Investment Company.[38]

During the last week of August 1941, Whitaker flew to Chicago, where he, Hamilton, and Hamilton's lawyer, Anan

Raymond, prepared four possible financing plans. Hamilton presented these options to Hixon in a five-hour conference the first week in September, and Hixon selected a plan that called for an initial investment of approximately $100,000.[39]

At 3:30 p.m. on Sept. 15, 1941, the principals of the new venture, named Aero-Marine Products, met at the law offices of Lindabury, Depue and Faulks on Broad Street in Newark, New Jersey. The first order of business was to elect officers for the new company. Robert Hixon was named president, Stephen Buchanan became vice president, Uncas A. Whitaker became vice president and treasurer, and Cleve J. Fredricksen became assistant treasurer. Whitaker had hired Fredricksen as the accountant for his new venture on the recommendation of American Machine and Foundry comptroller George Ingalls. Fredricksen spent the rest of his career with the company and eventually became chairman of AMP.[40]

The 7,000 shares of stock were distributed: Hixon and Midland Investment Company received all 2,000 shares of preferred stock at $46.60 per share and 3,000 shares of common stock at $1 per share; Buchanan received 2,000

Born on September 15, 1941, the original stock of Aero-Marine Products was split between Whitaker, Hixon and Midland, and Stephen Buchanan.

shares of common stock; Whitaker received 1,998 shares of common stock; and Carl Hamilton and R. Miles Warner each received one share of common stock.[41]

Al Curtis, who worked for Buchanan on the shop floor and eventually became advertising and sales promotion manager before leaving Whitaker's company in 1988, remembered the day the takeover happened:

> "I had worked there for about a year, and one day a tall, lanky individual walked in and announced that we were no longer Industrial Manufacturers. We were now Aero-Marine Products and instead of being paid in little envelopes, with dollar bills tucked in them, we were now being paid by check. So everybody immediately took off and dashed off to the nearest bank to see if the checks were any good. And that fella, of course, was Cleve Fredricksen."[42]

In the first year of operation, the new company began its never-ending task of educating customers on the benefits of solderless terminals by printing a glossy pamphlet listing their features and advantages.

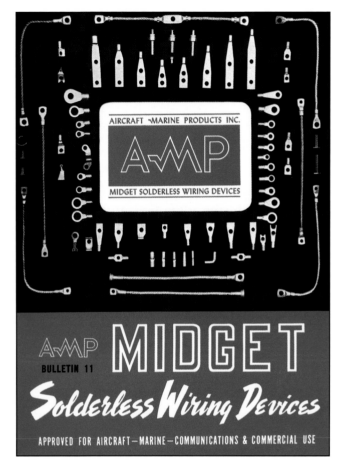

A-MP Solderless
WIRING DEVICES

WIRE TERMINALS
WITHOUT INSULATION SUPPORT

CATALOG SECTION 20

"PRECISION ENGINEERING APPLIED TO THE END OF A WIRE"

STANDARD (B)

FLAG TYPE

AIRCRAFT-MARINE PRODUCTS INC. 1523 N. FOURTH ST, HARRISBURG, PA.

A-MP's product line steadily grew throughout the war years as the company perfected both its products and its marketing.

CHAPTER TWO

SETTING THE STAGE

1941–1946

"Whitaker's idea, expressed through Carlson, was that in a couple of years we wanted to be head and shoulders above any of our competitors. ... So we delved into the engineering of a terminal."

— Tom Freedom[1]

ONE OF THE FIRST things to happen to the young company was a name change. U.A. Whitaker felt that Aero-Marine Products was too close to that of an existing firm, Aeromarine Insurance. After considering more than 100 new names, he settled on Aircraft-Marine Products, Inc.[2]

The company headed into World War II in need of bigger facilities, more production capabilities and more people.[3] The original office was located in a converted stucco house at 470 Rahway Avenue in Elizabeth, New Jersey, with a small production facility staffed by 24 workers in the Bayway Terminal Building. Whitaker found better office accommodations at 286 North Broad Street in Elizabeth, above a Greek restaurant, and soon opened a research and development lab in a rented storefront in nearby Westfield.

Nearly all of the company's manufacturing was done by subcontractors, the most significant being the Edwin Stimpson Company of Brooklyn, which made all the company's stampings for terminals and lugs.[4] Late in 1941, to supplement Stimpson, Whitaker contracted with Paul Shepperd, owner of a factory in Glen Rock, Pennsylvania, just south of York. Whitaker was familiar with the town from his American Machine and Foundry days, when AMF had its Glen Mixer Division there, and he liked the area.

The landscape reminded him of the rural Midwest, where he was raised, and the local workers seemed to adhere to a traditional work ethic. This latter quality was of particular importance to Whitaker at a time when labor relations in heavily unionized urban areas, like northern New Jersey, threatened the stability of manufacturing operations.[5]

Finding qualified personnel was more difficult than finding space, as good engineers were in short supply and great demand in the early 1940s. Fortunately, the connections Whitaker had made and the respect he had gained thus far in his career helped him find the right people.

One of Whitaker's earliest men, Dr. Frank Wells, had hired Whitaker for Westinghouse Air Brake in 1923 and later worked with him at American Machine and Foundry, where the two became friends.[6] Wells became Aircraft-Marine's first director of Research.

Wells, in turn, put Whitaker in touch with Dr. William S. Watts, an engineering professor at Tri-State College in Angola, Indiana, who ran an engineering consulting business on the side. While researching Industrial Manufacturers,

A-MP's Standard B terminals offered both strength and light weight.

Whitaker had hired Watts to conduct a survey of existing terminal manufacturers and subsequently hired him as an engineer.

Watts, in turn, recruited a bright young Tri-State graduate named Ken Neijstrom, who was working at Bendix. Although Neijstrom did not officially come on board until January 1942, he actually began working on engineering concepts for Aircraft-Marine in the fall of 1941.[7]

In October, Whitaker hired an old Hoover acquaintance, Vern Carlson, who had since moved to the Eureka Company, as his first director of Experimental Engineering. Whitaker also hired three other engineers from Eureka and wrote to Carl Hamilton that he had gotten "the four best out of a group of 60."[8]

It should be noted that raiding companies for personnel was not Whitaker's style, nor was it an accepted practice in the 1940s. As retired A-MP executive Leon Whipple later explained, "In those days, you didn't steal employees from the parent company."[9] Whitaker, the most scrupulous of businessmen, had hired the Eureka contingent based on a report, which later proved false, that the company was going out of business.[10]

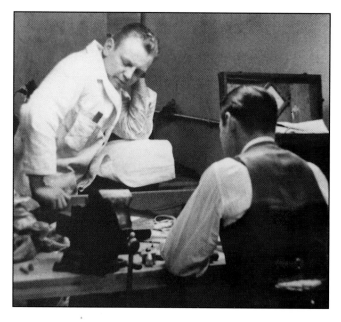

Shown in the Westfield, New Jersey, lab with George Coss (right), Ken Neijstrom (left) helped develop some of A-MP's earliest products.

It was through Carlson that Whitaker learned of G. Earle Walker, a former Eureka sales manager, a man who would play a pivotal

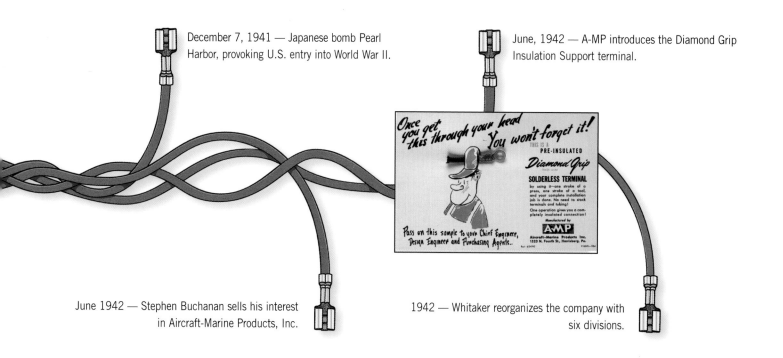

December 7, 1941 — Japanese bomb Pearl Harbor, provoking U.S. entry into World War II.

June, 1942 — A-MP introduces the Diamond Grip Insulation Support terminal.

June 1942 — Stephen Buchanan sells his interest in Aircraft-Marine Products, Inc.

1942 — Whitaker reorganizes the company with six divisions.

role in the evolution of the company's sales organization. Walker had left Eureka to work for the Crosley Company but in the fall of 1941 was looking for a new position. Carlson was impressed with Walker's sales acumen and recommended him to Whitaker, who talked Walker into taking a temporary position with Aircraft-Marine in December 1941.[11]

By this time, Whitaker had serious misgivings about Stephen Buchanan's capabilities in his self-appointed role as sales engineer. Walker's hire would help bring things to a head.

Buchanan Leaves the Company

As Whitaker became immersed in the day-to-day operations of the company, he began to realize Stephen Buchanan's shortcomings as a businessman. A clash between the two men was inevitable.

Buchanan had almost nothing in common with Whitaker's core team of professionals. Directors Robert Hixon and Miles Warner, for example, were graduates of Yale and Princeton, respectively, and Whitaker himself held engineering degrees from MIT and Carnegie Tech and a law degree from Cleveland Law School. Buchanan had a background as an electrician, inventor and field salesman, while the new leadership had technical and theoretical expertise and vast experience at high-level management, organization and finance.

Although Whitaker recognized that Buchanan was a skillful engineer with a certain amount of creativity and ambition, it was Buchanan's shoot-from-the-hip approach to sales and field engineering that created the biggest rift in the new company. Engineer Ken Neijstrom recalled, "He'd go out and meet customers and commit us to make something, like 10 million terminals or some damn thing, and we didn't even know what the hell the design was going to be. He had it all up here [in his head]."[12]

Cleve Fredricksen, who handled financial affairs for Aircraft-Marine and would become chairman, characterized Buchanan as "a traveling salesman who had a bag of tricks in each pocket. ... He was an inventive engineer who would call on customers, sell them things, carry orders in his pocket, and many times forget to turn them in."[13]

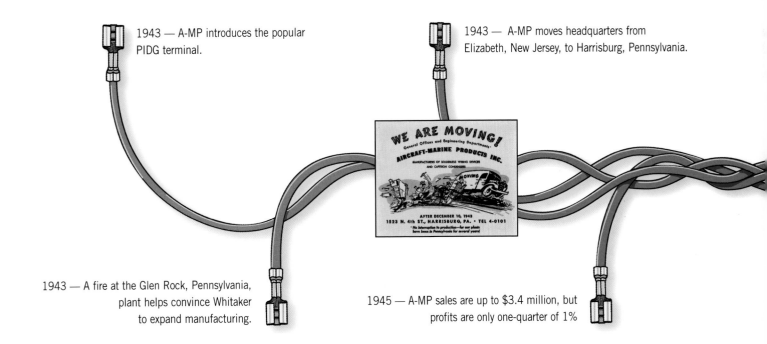

1943 — A-MP introduces the popular PIDG terminal.

1943 — A-MP moves headquarters from Elizabeth, New Jersey, to Harrisburg, Pennsylvania.

1943 — A fire at the Glen Rock, Pennsylvania, plant helps convince Whitaker to expand manufacturing.

1945 — A-MP sales are up to $3.4 million, but profits are only one-quarter of 1%

Because Buchanan saw himself as the company's chief salesman, Whitaker's appointment of Walker as the new sales manager probably served as the handwriting on the wall. In June 1942, Buchanan approached Whitaker about selling his interest in the company, and Whitaker immediately began drawing up a plan. By July 1942, Buchanan had resigned from the company and sold his stock to the directors and Midland Investment Company.[14]

The Evolution of the Solderless Terminal

From the moment Aircraft-Marine was formed, Whitaker established research and development as a top priority and immediately began looking for ways to improve the company's products for its chief customer, the wartime aircraft industry.

Although solderless terminal technology had been around for years, the terminals themselves were still relatively primitive in 1941. Aircraft-Marine's first A-Type terminals consisted of a barrel turned out on ordinary shop equipment and then riveted to a tongue stamping. The first crimping tools were little more than modified pliers.

Under Whitaker's supervision, the A-Type terminal was refined by a one-piece construction of the terminal body and the addition of a thin metal sleeve to strengthen the terminal where it was crimped. Soon, the tongue was streamlined, the barrel shortened and the crimping improved. This next line of terminals, the Standard B (named for its shape), became Aircraft-Marine's first bread-and-butter product and the basis from which other refinements grew.[15]

Tom Freedom, who was hired as an engineer-draftsman in February 1942 and was involved in the early development of terminals, described in a 1996 interview the engineering approach that was to become A-MP's legacy.

"Whitaker's idea, expressed through Carlson, was that in a couple of years we wanted to be head and shoulders above any of our competitors, which were Thomas & Betts, and Burndy. They made massive terminals, put together with screw machine parts. They were too heavy. So we

Tom Freedom, shown conducting a seminar on terminal construction, was hired in 1942 and went on to help develop the Pre-Insulated Diamond Grip terminal, one of the early bread-and-butter products.

delved into the engineering of a terminal. And there was something that got missed by everyone but A-MP. There's a rule in electrical engineering that says a conductor has to have a cross-section of so many circular mils in order to conduct a certain amount of current without burning up. But we were able to bypass that a little bit and make our terminals a lot lighter. Because in actual use, you put a terminal on the end of a wire. It's not going to sit there in mid-air and conduct current. The terminal is going to be attached to something, and the wire is going to go somewhere. So both the terminal and the wire become conductors of heat. The heat dissipates back along the wire, down through the brass stud or whatever the wire is attached to. Therefore, we could make the terminal metal a little thinner and get away with it. That's what sold us to the aircraft companies — the lighter weight."[16]

The Standard B terminal did have its limitations. Aircraft-Marine's own catalog recommended the product for applications "where vibration is not a serious factor and there is little strain of insulation where wire meets terminal barrel."[17]

In June 1942, Aircraft-Marine introduced the Diamond Grip Insulation Support terminal, which represented the first real breakthrough in terminals designed for operation under stress. It immediately became a big seller with aircraft manufacturers, who were naturally concerned about the performance of terminals under the most severe conditions.

Aircraft-Marine was not alone in offering a terminal with "insulation support," which was simply an extended outer barrel that supported the wire where it entered the terminal. However, Aircraft-Marine's product had innovative design features that put it ahead of the competition. For one thing, it was shorter and more compact than other terminals. And

Above: The Diamond Grip terminal, in an early advertisement, could be crimped more securely because of its notched design.

Left: With Earle Walker in charge of sales in 1943, A-MP's message of "precision engineering" and cost-effectiveness was hammered home.

The problem of making quick, sure, electrical connections has been met and solved by the complete line of AMP Terminals.

We have incorporated basic features into many varied designs to meet the specifications of the major users of solderless terminals. Aircraft type terminals differ in many respects from Marine type, just as terminals for communications are unlike those used in commercial installations.

Underlying these differences of design required by varying usage, are the AMP principles of manufacture and installation. Every AMP terminal, regardless of its individual specifications, is produced under the rigid standards of quality and performance set up in our own plant—the result of intensive research and product development, coupled with wide practical experience of user requirements.

As a result, AMP terminals are not only approved from use by the proper authorities, they are specified by many companies as the preferred type of solderless wiring connection.

the inside of the barrel featured a notched design — the so-called "diamond grip" — that allowed a more secure crimp.

Not long after the diamond grip, Aircraft-Marine introduced the Pre-Insulated Diamond Grip Terminal (PIDG) in 1943. It featured a piece of insulation already attached to the barrel of the terminal and was destined to become a huge seller.

Neijstrom recalled that the idea for the product was suggested by the Glenn L. Martin aircraft company, which was buying Aircraft-Marine's insulation support terminals and adding a piece of insulation to them at its own plant.[18] However, Whitaker himself also had apparently seen this practice during a West Coast visit to a Boeing factory and returned with the idea of pre-attaching insulation.[19]

Tom Freedom, who helped design the PIDG, recalled that one of the challenges was finding the right plastic for the insulation. "Plastics were in their infancy. It was a problem to get a plastic that would bind to the barrel, as well as hold up to voltage breakdown, and not crack and loosen when you crimped it," he said.[20]

Along with the PIDG, A-MP engineers developed the CERTI-CRIMP TOOL, a ratcheted plier that virtually guaranteed secure terminal installation, since the jaws of the tool could not be reopened until a proper crimp had been applied.

A-MP had created both a better terminal and a better way to apply it, two innovations that were crucial to the defense industry at a time when production demands required both reliability and speed of installation in electrical connections.

Reorganizing the Company

The development of these products came none too soon for Whitaker's fledgling company. In its second month of existence, Aircraft-Marine recorded a sales volume of $54,000, but the total dropped to $47,000 the next month and plunged to $16,000 in December 1941.[21] The first quarter of 1942 was

not much better, with the company averaging less than $40,000 for each of the first three months.[22]

The problem was not a shortage of markets. With the bombing of Pearl Harbor on December 7, 1941, the United States was officially at war and was producing record numbers of planes, ships and tanks, all of which needed electrical connectors. Rather, the sales lag resulted largely from a combination of factors that Whitaker worked furiously to correct.

First was the company's general lack of structure. Early in 1942, Whitaker completely reorganized the company, creating six divisions: Financial, Sales, Engineering, Patent and Legal, Production, and Inspection. Among the hand-picked leaders of these divisions were men who would figure prominently in Aircraft-Marine's

---

Determined to stay current with technology, A-MP engineers turned out products to meet every possible application and wiring need of the 1940s. The product catalog quickly grew to thousands of parts.

A-MP AND THE SUPERFORTRESS

IN LESS THAN A MONTH, Germany demonstrated what overwhelming air power could do. In the September 1939 Luftwaffe attacks on Poland, Europe and America watched in uncomfortable disbelief as the Polish defense was easily overwhelmed from the sky. America was forced to recognize that it had nothing to stand up to that kind of air power.

"Germany put more planes in the air in one raid over Poland than we have in our entire air force," reported U.S. Army colonels Tooey Spaatz and George Kenney, who were observing in Europe.[1]

Again in 1940, the German Blitzkrieg — lightning war — rolled over Denmark and Norway, and beginning in May, successfully defeated the Netherlands, Belgium and France.

In open support of the Allies but not willing to commit to war, President Franklin D. Roosevelt on May 16, 1940, called for U.S. production of 50,000 planes per year. Mobilization on this scale strained every resource of the major airframe manufacturers, for it demanded they build planes not only at an unheard-of volume but also to the higher standard of performance and reliability required in combat.

A-MP's development of solderless terminals could not have come at a better time — they could be applied faster than soldered terminals and at lower cost. Furthermore, because they were made from stamped metal rather than screw machine parts, they were considerably lighter than standard terminals. They found their way into the production lines of many military aircraft, including the Glenn Martin Company's B-26.

However, by 1941, the U.S. military was well aware that its flagship bomber, the B-17 "Flying Fortress," lacked the speed, range and altitude (the British called it the "Flying Target") required for long-range missions.

Major airframe manufacturers were invited to build a high-altitude superbomber capable of carrying a heavy payload of bombs at 400 mph and upwards of 30,000 feet. The bomber also would need a range of more than 5,000 miles. One glance at a world globe shows why. If Britain fell, American bombers would have to be able to reach Germany from the U.S.

Boeing, Consolidated, Douglas and Lockheed entered the superbomber competition, but only Boeing was able to deliver. (Douglas and Lockheed withdrew, and the Consolidated entry, the B-32, ran into design problems)[2].

The plane Boeing finally delivered in spring 1944 — the airplane most responsible for the defeat of Japan — was the legendary B-29 Superfortress. A-MP PIDG terminals and CERTI-CRIMP tools were used extensively in its production.

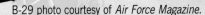

B-29 photo courtesy of *Air Force Magazine*.

As research and development expanded, A-MP knocked down walls in the Westfield, New Jersey, facility and grew to fill all four storefronts.

future. Whitaker himself took charge of the Engineering Division; Cleve Fredricksen headed the Financial Division; R.J. Szukala, a family friend of Miles Warner, headed the Patent and Legal Division; and G. Earle Walker was put in charge of Sales.[23]

Second was the problem of the sales organization itself, which Whitaker had already gone a long way toward solving when he hired the aggressive and inventive Walker. Still, Walker faced a daunting task. Not only was the existing sales organization chaotic and informal, but it faced an industry that was inexperienced in — and resistant to — solderless terminals. (Bill Watts reported in an April 1942 memo that one company was puzzled about how to solder Aircraft-Marine's solderless terminals onto wires!)[24] Walker saw the company's first need as educating the customer. However, he had no sales force and only a shoestring budget. Walker attacked the problem three ways: he created informative product brochures for sales repre-

sentatives to carry into the field; he launched a direct mail campaign to company presidents; and he initiated a national ad campaign which ran in all the leading trade publications.[25]

Aircraft-Marine's third major obstacle was competition from well-established companies. Chief among them was Thomas & Betts, a company founded in 1898 by two Princeton graduates, Robert Thomas and Hobart Betts. Beginning with an electrical conduit business in New York City, they expanded into electrical terminals and moved to Elizabeth, New Jersey, in 1917.[26] By the time Aircraft-Marine came on the scene, T&B was already 43 years old and had more than a decade head start in the solderless terminal business.

Whitaker's response to Thomas & Betts was simple: develop a superior product and, along with it, an improved crimping tool. Aircraft-Marine's terminals could be offered to the customer at a lower installed cost, a concept that was hammered home by Walker in his marketing thrusts.

All these moves — reorganization, new sales strategies and product development — soon paid off. By mid-1942, the Diamond Grip Insulation Support Terminal had established Aircraft-

Marine as a key supplier of terminals for defense contractors. Several large aircraft manufacturers, including Douglas and Vega (a subsidiary of Lockheed), converted to A-MP Diamond Grip terminals, and in June, A-MP joined Thomas & Betts as the only approved suppliers of terminals for Army tanks.[27]

Boeing also developed into a major account as the company expanded its production of long-range bombers. In 1940, the company had been awarded a contract to develop the B-29 Superfortress, a long-range, high-altitude bomber capable of flying 5,500 miles at a ceiling of 30,000 feet. Immediately after Pearl Harbor, Boeing accelerated production of B-29s, which were to become the Army Air Corps' principal heavy bomber.[28] Boeing used PIDG terminals and CERTI-CRIMP tools extensively in production.

Things began to turn around by the second quarter of 1942. In April, sales jumped to $60,000 a month, and by the end of the year Aircraft-Marine had revenue of more than $830,000. Even more impressive was the $500,000 backlog in orders amassed.[29]

The Move to Harrisburg

With the Diamond Grip Insulation Support terminals established as an industry standard and military aircraft production in full swing, business remained good in early 1943, as A-MP recorded sales of $500,000 for the first quarter alone.

Research and development work continued at the Central Avenue site in Westfield, where the company by this time had expanded into all four store fronts in the building, knocking down the walls between them.[30]

The increased demand for products, however, began to strain the production facilities in Elizabeth. In mid-1942, when orders started to increase dramatically, Whitaker contracted with Gaynor Electric, of Bridgeport, Connecticut, to manufacture terminals. This source supplemented A-MP's other two subcontractors, the Stimpson Company in Brooklyn and the plant in Glen Rock. The manufactured terminals were sent to the Bayway Terminal Building in Elizabeth for assembly, packing and shipping.

Still, by early 1943 the company needed to expand, and Whitaker was reluctant to do so in northern New Jersey. For one thing, the area was already a center of defense-related industries, so labor and suitable buildings were scarce. For another, Whitaker was uncomfortable with the labor union situation in the area.[31] He had good reason to be. In February, the 17,000 union workers of the Phelps Dodge plant right across the street from the Bayway building went out on a wildcat strike, taking Aircraft-Marine's 17 union employees with them.[32]

If Whitaker needed another incentive to decentralize his operations, it was provided in the form of a fire at Paul Shepperd's Glen Rock plant on May 21, 1943. Apparently ignited by a lightning strike during an early morning storm, the fire destroyed $75,000 worth of machinery and equipment.[33] Although no one was injured, the incident was a reminder of the need for multiple manufacturing sites. Al Curtis helped clean up the destroyed factory and remembered the extraordinary measures A-MP took to stay operating:

"We got word on Saturday night. Sunday, we called everybody and told them to get on a train or get in cars or buses or whatever. We salvaged

In early 1943, Whitaker moved the company to Harrisburg, Pennsylvania, where the headquarters are still located.

as much as we possibly could, cleaning up machinery and products. And then we took over any place we could get, including the homes of employees. We put machinery in their living rooms, where they went to work. We went around every day and picked up their products. It worked so well that I don't think more than half a dozen of our customers even knew that we were practically out of business."[34]

In October 1942, Whitaker called on Leon Whipple, a colleague from AMF, to scout sites in Pennsylvania, Connecticut and Ohio. Whipple was a tool and die man who Whitaker had used as a part-time consultant when Aircraft-Marine first started up, and Whitaker knew he had scouted locations for AMF.[35]

From Whipple's preliminary reports, Whitaker narrowed the search to eastern and central Pennsylvania, and in March 1943, he put R.J. Szukala in charge of the relocation effort. Szukala visited Reading and Scranton but rejected both for various reasons, and by March 18, the choice was again narrowed, this time to Lancaster, York and Harrisburg.[36]

Despite a chilly initial response from the Harrisburg Chamber of Commerce, the more Whitaker studied the location, the more attractive it looked. He already knew that area of Pennsylvania from visiting the Glen Rock plant and felt at home there, something Whipple remembered in a 1996 interview:

"When he went to American Machine and Foundry in the early days, there was a Glen Mixer Division down in Glen Rock, which he was in charge of, so he already had connections in the Harrisburg area. Another important reason was the fact that it wasn't too far from Long Level [a deep section of the Susquehanna River near York], and Whitaker liked to sail. The third reason [he felt at home] would probably be that he was a farm boy, and then and now Pennsylvania has the largest population of farms of any state in the

nation. Whitaker liked to hire farm-bred boys. I think he felt they were better workers."[37]

More importantly, Szukala's study showed that Harrisburg had a sizeable labor force of skilled tool and die makers and that the city was a transportation hub with rail access to the major urban centers in the East and Midwest. Finally, Szukala found the city itself inviting, with its state government complex and downtown accommodations.[38]

In mid-March 1943, Szukala looked at a vacant automobile dealership at 1521-31 North Fourth Street in Harrisburg. By June, negotiations were complete to lease the building with an option to buy, and by December 10, Aircraft-Marine had moved from Elizabeth into its new headquarters.[39] The move to Harrisburg would, of course, prove to be one of the most significant events in A-MP's history. Company headquarters

Whitaker, inset, settled into his new office, located in a vacant automobile dealership on North Fourth Street in downtown Harrisburg, in early 1943.

remained there from 1943 to 1951 and have since expanded to a modern, sprawling campus just east of the city.

One of the first important results of the new move was that Aircraft-Marine began fabricating its own terminals, reducing its reliance on outside contractors. Ken Neijstrom, who was put in charge of setting up the new plant on Fourth Street, recalled the incident that spurred A-MP's first venture into manufacturing.

"There was a company in Long Island City, the Bates Company, that made what we called the Navy terminal. They couldn't keep up with us. Our production manager was always complaining about this company because they were always behind on that terminal. So I said to him one day, 'Why don't you get that die in here and we'll see if we can run it.' Since we had paid for the die, we got a hold of it, and we

bought a press and set it up to make the Navy terminal. One of our efficiency men figured out how much we saved by doing it ourselves, and that sort of started us from one terminal to another terminal."[40]

A-MP at the End of the War

Sales were strong throughout the war, but profits were minimal. A-MP finished 1943 with a sales volume reaching $2.2 million. Sales continued to increase, to $2.6 million in 1944 and $3.4 million in 1945, but the company's profit margin was just 1 percent after taxes in 1944 and one-quarter of 1 percent in 1945. Several factors contributed to this situation, including the expense of moving to Harrisburg and tooling up for in-house manufacture of products, along with the large federal tax on profits.[41]

So despite the steady flow of business, A-MP found itself in need of financing during the middle 1940s. The end of the war was near and the company soon would have to convert from defense to commercial markets, which would require capital. Toward this end, Whitaker received a loan of $150,000 from Dolphin Deposit Trust, a local Harrisburg bank, in 1944. A few months later, Midland Investment Company agreed to purchase $55,000 of a promisory note in addition to buying more stock. Finally, in 1945, AMP secured a loan for up to $500,000 from the Federal Reserve Bank in Philadelphia.[42]

Wartime production had been good for A-MP by opening up markets, but Whitaker learned a valuable lesson: Avoid doing business with the government whenever possible. Although he was a patriot and always willing to donate company research toward national defense, he found the government, with its tangle of regulations and bureaucracies, to be a frustrating and meddlesome customer. Bills were scrutinized to the penny by government bean counters, who held up payment for minor accounting mistakes, even when the mistake benefited the government.

"When and if this war ever ends, I certainly want to get into a business where I would never be required to sell the government anything," he told Bill Watts. It was a prescient statement.[43]

A-MP's answer for the post-war era of automation was the Automatic Wire Terminator, which it installed without charge for large customers.

CHAPTER THREE

THE PROBLEM WITH PEACE

1946–1950

"I think we're doing the right thing. I have all the confidence in the world that automatic machines can be a good product area for this company."

— Joe Brenner, 1996, recalling comment from 1947[1]

THE END OF THE war meant opportunity for A-MP, but it wasn't going to happen overnight. U.A. Whitaker had no great love for government contracts, but the fact remained that they had propelled his company from virtually no business to millions of dollars in sales in only a few years. But after the war A-MP's biggest customer canceled most of its military contracts. Postwar conversion to a consumer market proved to be a painful and lengthy process, but A-MP was not alone. Many businesses had to wean themselves from wartime military contracts by downsizing workforces and retooling for peacetime products.

Aircraft-Marine also went through a period of austerity and drastic cutbacks in personnel. As Cleve Fredricksen remembered: "All of sudden you were way up here, then victory in Europe and the Japanese surrendered, and zoom, you were way down here. Now you've still got receivables, but people aren't really anxious to pay."[2]

But two decades of pent-up consumerism were about to be unleashed in a tremendous boom of industry and prosperity. Despite the pain, A-MP worked to position itself not on the front lines and store shelves, but inside every appliance and gadget that Americans would soon crave.

Lean Times

By mid-1946, less than two years after securing its V-loan from the Federal Reserve, the company again found itself in need of cash. At the July 6, 1946, board of directors meeting, Whitaker explained, "In order to complete the reconversion to postwar business, provide inventory necessary for new product lines, pay current taxes and reduce the loan at the Federal Reserve Bank as required, new financing in the amount of $350,000 will be required."[3]

Midland Investment Company once again came to AMP's aid. In 1946, it purchased a promissory note of $200,000.[4]

Even with the infusion of money, A-MP faced a variety of pressing problems. Postwar material shortages — especially of copper and steel — were a problem from the manufacturing side. A-MP, which by this time made about 3,000 products, could not stockpile enough material to maintain inventories and fill all customer orders promptly. Also, many of A-MP's customers were

---

Throughout the late 1940s, the Diamond Grip and Standard B terminals continued to sell in huge quantities.

cutting back on production, which translated into fewer orders for terminals and other components.

Labor unrest immediately after the war spread across the country as workers demanded higher wages. Nationwide strikes in the steel and railroad industries, and at the plants of several of A-MP's large customers, further slowed post-war production in key areas.[5]

The only way for A-MP to survive the year 1946 was to severely reduce the payroll. About 70 percent of the sales staff and 30 percent of the engineering department were laid off. Tom Freedom recalled that Whitaker did everything possible to retain people through hard times.

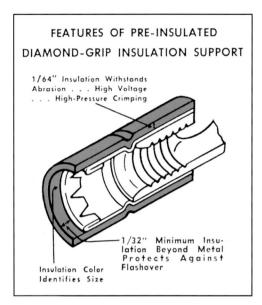

FEATURES OF PRE-INSULATED DIAMOND-GRIP INSULATION SUPPORT

1/64" Insulation Withstands Abrasion . . . High Voltage . . . High-Pressure Crimping

1/32" Minimum Insulation Beyond Metal Protects Against Flashover

Insulation Color Identifies Size

"A-MP had a big heart. Whitaker established that, it was part of his whole being. Of course, there was a certain amount of weeding out of dead wood. But, for the valued employees, Whitaker tried everything — he'd reduce the work week, reduce the work day, ask people to take a week's vacation without pay, in order to keep them on the payroll. It cut back on us, but we hung on."[6]

In fact, A-MP had a progressive approach to labor from the beginning. As early as 1944, the company pursued group insurance for employees. By the late 1940s, it was offering six paid holidays annually and had established an incentive plan and grievance procedure. In 1949, it initiated a pension plan.[7]

Whitaker had always cultivated a strong, open relationship between labor and management. This

Education was critical to A-MP's success as the company steadily won converts among reticent manufacturers.

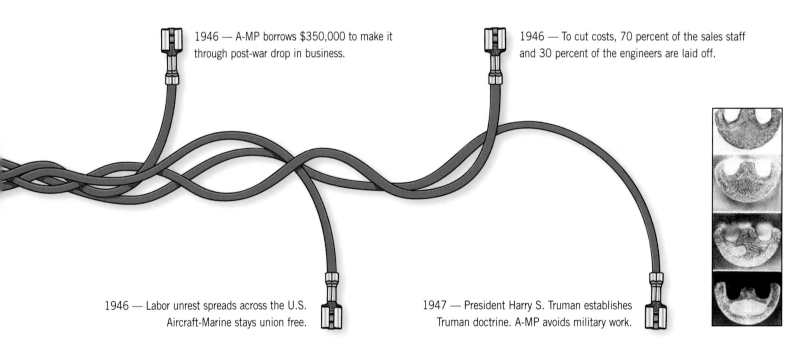

1946 — A-MP borrows $350,000 to make it through post-war drop in business.

1946 — To cut costs, 70 percent of the sales staff and 30 percent of the engineers are laid off.

1946 — Labor unrest spreads across the U.S. Aircraft-Marine stays union free.

1947 — President Harry S. Truman establishes Truman doctrine. A-MP avoids military work.

approach was surely an outgrowth of his general respect and concern for people, but it also was a practical hedge against the labor unrest of the day. His plan was to find good people and offer them a better work environment and benefit package than could be found in a union shop.[8]

In a report to Whitaker in October 1946, personnel department head R.J. Szukala wrote:

"The company has made a special effort to hire stable, loyal and industrious people for its organization. The result has been a most satisfactory labor/management relationship with mutual confidence and respect for each other. The employees have not joined any labor organization and

Hand tools made it easy for novices to guarantee a perfect wire/terminal connection every time.

have an attitude of mutual cooperation for the success of the company."[9]

Automation

Throughout the late 1940s, A-MP was supported by the General Products Division, which turned out the familiar Standard B terminal, Pre-Insulated Diamond Grip terminal and CERTI-CRIMP tool. Furthermore, Whitaker and his engi-

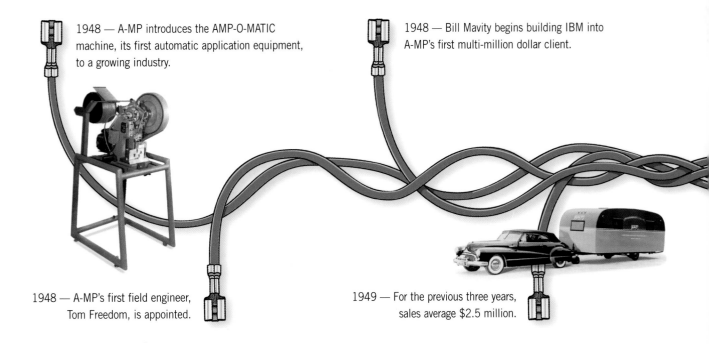

1948 — A-MP introduces the AMP-O-MATIC machine, its first automatic application equipment, to a growing industry.

1948 — Bill Mavity begins building IBM into A-MP's first multi-million dollar client.

1948 — A-MP's first field engineer, Tom Freedom, is appointed.

1949 — For the previous three years, sales average $2.5 million.

neers already had discovered the key that unlocked the door to a vast market: lower installed cost. Offer a customer both a superior product and the means to install it, and that business was a customer for life.

Automatic machinery was the next logical step in the concept of lower applied costs. Automation had the potential to dramatically reduce installed cost, and Whitaker foresaw its potential with big customers like General Electric and IBM, which were gearing up to mass-produce consumer products.[10] Reflecting on automation, Chet Timmins, who worked in the Automachine Division and would later become a vice president, said, "Application tooling has been pivotal to the success of A-MP because it allowed the A-MP sales organization to sell the applied cost story."[11]

Machine development had begun in 1945 and involved two technical phases. First, the terminals themselves had to be manufactured in continuous strip form — like paper dolls — that could be stored on a reel. Second, a machine had to be developed that could feed this reel through an applicator or die that crimped each terminal onto the end of a wire and then cut it off. General Electric began testing A-MP's earliest machines in its Fort Wayne, Indiana, plant as early as November 1945. By 1946, IBM and several other customers also were considering the system.[12]

The machines and strip-form terminals officially went on the market in 1948. The first model, the AMP-O-MATIC, was a bench-mounted pneumatic machine operated by foot pedal that was capable of applying about 1,000 terminals per hour, depending on the operator. It could easily be detached and moved around a plant. A-MP loaned the machines to customers who bought a minimum of 50,000 terminals per year.

As was so often the case in A-MP's history, the success of the Automachine Division can be traced to astute personnel decisions. The division's first head was Frank Pierce, an engineer who had worked with Whitaker at Hoover and moved on to Eureka. (In fact, Whitaker himself had recommended Pierce for the Eureka job vacated by Vern Carlson when Carlson was hired by A-MP.)[13]

Other key players in Automachine included Joseph Brenner (who went on to become A-MP's CEO and chairman), and Bill Pollock, who would head the division before moving up the corporate ladder. The ingenious Quentin Berg also worked in Automachines before leaving A-MP to start his own company.

Brenner was literally recruited off the street. A native of nearby Carlisle, Pennsylvania, Brenner held a bachelor's degree from Dickinson College and an MBA from Harvard and had some experience in manufacturing. In 1946 he was fresh out of the Navy and looking for a job. One day he was in Harrisburg walking by A-MP's Fourth Street plant when a friend who worked there, Joe Wintergrass, stuck his head out the door and hailed him, saying he ought to apply at A-MP. One thing led to another, and Brenner landed a job in the Engineering Department.

At the time, the General Products Division was the big revenue producer for A-MP, and the engineers there viewed the automatic machine project with some skepticism, Brenner said. "We were the Johnny-come-latelies, and they looked over at what we were doing and said, 'Well, maybe ...'"[14]

Nonetheless, the division crackled with a free exchange of ideas. The relationship between management and engineers was loose and per-

Above: A-MP Power Presses could terminate more than 3,000 wires per hour.

Right: Terminals were stamped in continuous strips and provided to customers on reels.

Above: Blair Paules demonstrating a new hydraulic tool. L-R: Tom Freedom, Kemper "Crimper" Hammell, George Ritter, Vern Carlson, Blair Paules, Jack Thompson, Joseph Brenner, Bill Pollock

Below: Ever meticulous and creative, Whitaker kept a notebook in 1948 that contains sketches and his observations.

sonal. Pierce, the division head, worked "plunk in the middle" of the other engineers rather than in a private office off to himself, according to Dick Leuba, an apprentice engineer at the time.[15]

Brenner vividly recalled his first encounter with Pierce and Quentin Berg.

"[Pierce] said, 'You're going to work for Quentin Berg. We all call him Ice.' I said fine. He introduced me to Ice, we shook hands, and I said, 'Ice, what would you like me to do?' He said, 'This is my desk. I'm moving off it to that board over there. ... You're going to be at this desk and you do everything that I'm not doing — that's your assignment.'"[16]

A few years later, Pierce had moved on and both Brenner and Bill Pollock were up for the job. Brenner remembered how Whitaker handled the situation as he tried to settle who would become the new division head:

"Whit called us both into his office and said, 'You're both qualified for this job of being the head of the Automachine Division. Joe, you've done a good job for us. Bill, you've done good work. I've got two good men, well qualified. Which one of you is going to take it? Either one of you is fine with me.' I said, 'Bill is the more accomplished engineer. I think he should do it, and I'll be glad to

be his assistant.' And [Whitaker] said, 'That's fine. That solves my problem.'"[17]

Other Products

While A-MP was developing its automatic machines in the mid- and late 1940s, the number of terminals and hand tools continued to swell. By the end of the decade, the company was selling a whole array of products.

Among the many terminals offered by A-MP in the 1940s was the Solistrand, for use on solid wire, which Freedom had originally developed for General Electric during the war. The need for this product arose because A-MP's standard cross crimp was not effective on solid wire. After much

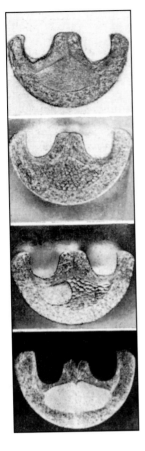

experiment, Freedom came up with the W-crimp (or double indent), so named because of its shape in cross section.

"Whereas A-MP's cross crimp went across the terminal, I went longitudinal with the terminal, so it folded in on each side of the wire. That one would hold up on solid wire. We had to convince customers who were skeptical of it. We'd put it in a tensile machine and pull and pull and pull. The terminals would remain in the jaws but the wire would break. It wouldn't pull out of the terminal."[18]

Above left & right: A folding double crimp guaranteed connection with solid or stranded wires, or a combination of both.

Below: A-MP developed a patented anti-corrosion process for corrosive environments.

The Solistrand proved equally effective on stranded wire or combinations of stranded and solid wire. Another innovation, the Knife-Disconnect, allowed quick and easy connection and disconnection of two wires for applications such as harnesses and electronic components.

During the 1940s, A-MP engineers also developed a patented corrosion-proofing procedure for terminals used in corrosive environments, such as aboard ships where salt attacks the strength of metal, or in laboratories.

Along with these advances in terminals came a steady stream of innovations in hand tools, including the CERTI-CRIMP, new models of commercial tools with compound leverage jaws and hydraulics, and combination tools for home use that could both strip wire and crimp terminals.

The Guns or Butter Debate

As the company steadily expanded its product portfolio, conflict was brewing between Whitaker and G. Earle Walker, the sales manager hired for his marketing expertise. The two men had clashed over several issues, including whether A-MP should concentrate on military or commercial markets.

Although World War II was over, the Cold War was just beginning. In 1947, President Harry S. Truman, in response to growing tensions with the USSR about ideology and spheres of influence, had established the Truman Doctrine, in which the United States pledged to "support free peoples who are resisting attempted subjugation by armed minorities or by outside pressures." The doctrine would be used to justify sending aid and troops abroad, including to Korea in 1950.[19]

As America once again built up its military might, Walker sensed the potential market and tracked reports in the press and trade publications. He urged Whitaker to pursue government contracts, mentioning queries he had received about clearance to work on guided missiles and nuclear weapons.[20]

But Whitaker was leery. He disliked dealing with the government and wanted to avoid a return to anything near the level of dependence on government contracts that A-MP had experienced during World War II. Looking for advice, Whitaker asked Brenner for his opinion.

Brenner said he replied, "Well, I think we're doing the right thing. I have all the confidence in the world that automatic machines can be a good product area for this company."[21]

Whitaker responded that Walker thought the military had more potential.

"No, I can't agree with that," Brenner recalled saying. "Commercial is the way we should go."

Whitaker, of course, readily agreed, and that was the end of the conversation. Reflecting later on that moment, Brenner said, "That was a major decision in the life of a company. And they all start small."[22]

Walker and Whitaker also disagreed about which was the cart and which the horse: sales or engineering. Walker, the marketing man, believed that engineering existed to support sales, whereas Whitaker, the engineer, believed the reverse.

This A-MP booth was set up at a tradeshow on Chicago's Navy Pier in the late 1940s. From here, salesmen could easily attract new customers.

Walker would become incensed by every sale lost because of a product that didn't meet a customer's specifications or an order that couldn't be filled because of inventory backlogs. In a 1988 interview, Walker said, "I regarded every sale as lost virginity or something. An engineer can get back a drawing, but a salesman can't get back a lost sale."[23]

Whitaker was less concerned about minor setbacks, confident that customers would be drawn back to a superior product.[24]

Despite their disagreements, the two men maintained a good relationship. According to Walker, "We didn't disagree violently, you understand, but rather in a pleasant, affable manner. I needed him and he needed me."[25]

The two men were bound to disagree simply because of their very different personalities. Dottie Yingling worked with both men in the earliest days of the company and went on to receive the prestigious A-MP Distinguished Leadership Impact Award in 1993 for her wide-ranging roles in the company. She remembered the contrast well:

"Mr. Walker, he had to have a very elegant office with his own private bathroom and everything, and Whit didn't want anything like that. But his buddies refused to allow him to have an office that wasn't at least as good as Mr. Walker's. He always hated it because he never wanted any special privileges of any kind. ... He was really quite a wonderful man. ... Walker, however, was very different from the other men.

He was impeccably dressed. Whereas Whitaker drove an old beat-up Ford to work, he drove a Cadillac. He needed a lot of attention and he got a lot of attention, and he turned out to be quite a genius in developing a sales organization."[26]

In truth, the two could not function without each other, and Walker and Whitaker took steps in 1948 to bring their functions into harmony. By that time, A-MP's increasingly technical products and its policy of developing terminals specifically for customers' needs had created a knowledge gap. Whitaker's solution? Field engineers. Tom Freedom was the first.

"That was a traumatic problem for me. I loved the inventing and design work. But by that time we had enough different products on the market that they asked me to go out in the field to back up sales. ... I didn't want to do it. I went all the way up to Whitaker, cryin' the blues. He said 'Tom, you can't invent 'em all. We need you out there now. There's a pressing need to have the customer's personnel trained.'"[27]

Freedom flew to plants in a three-seat Piper PA-12 with an AMP-O-MATIC strapped on the seat behind him. He would drive to plants and hold seminars on hand tools and terminals. In time, more personnel were added and Freedom became chief of field engineers.

Morgan Prentiss drove this convertible Buick A-MP display trailer as a sales trainee. Prentiss later rose to a global marketing position.

Field engineers and direct salesmen evolved as the foundation of Walker's sales force. From the outset he had recognized the ineffectiveness of using jobbers or distributors. As the company was learning, selling solderless terminals required educating customers, most of whom were still ignorant or skeptical about crimp technology. This was a task distributors were not equipped to do. While training salesmen, Walker emphasized the need to get down on the factory floor. "You don't sell the purchasing agent. You sell the electrical engineer or the mechanical engineer. ... Above all, you must, as a salesman, get down on the production line so that you're sure the foreman likes your product."[28]

Sel Friedlander, who went on to become A-MP's director of Corporate Staff Services, began in 1948 in Chicago, working part-time as a clerk for Ed Hefter, whom Walker had hired as the company's Midwestern sales representative. Friedlander remembered salesmen carrying shoeboxes of sample terminals around to plants. "The manufacturing engineer was the key to our success. He understood the applied cost. The purchasing agent was the last guy we went to."[29]

A-MP's most successful salesman of the late 1940s was probably the legendary Bill Mavity. Walker had worked with Mavity at Philadelphia Electric and considered him the consummate salesman. Mavity was assigned as Aircraft-Marine's manufacturer's rep for upstate New York and New England, with General Electric his main account.

When Walker decided to take over GE as a house account, he offered Mavity IBM in exchange. A-MP had been doing business with IBM since 1942, but the orders had been modest: $1,500 in 1942 and $500 in 1943. Mavity built it into a multimillion dollar customer and made himself wealthy along the way.[30]

The Late 1940s in Perspective

From the perspective of later years, the late 1940s can be viewed as a staging ground for what was to come. They were not particularly profitable years. Sales averaged just below $2.5 million for 1946 through 1949, a drop from the wartime peak of $3.4 million in 1945. Profits did inch up to an average of about 4 percent during this period.[31]

But perhaps more significant than its mere survival of the postwar recession was the fact that right through the slack times, Aircraft-Marine continued to push ahead with the development of the technology — terminals, automated machinery and application tooling — that would position it to cash in on the coming boom in consumer goods.

A-MP engineers in the drafting department in 1950. The company was known for its engineering culture.

CHAPTER FOUR

A-MP TAKES OFF

THE EARLY 1950s

"I challenged them to come up with a good harness that would be cheap enough for consumer goods and demonstrate that we could just plug into it. They loved the assignment."

— Dottie Yingling, 1996[1]

A-MP HAD SPENT the last years of the 1940s jockeying for position in the consumer market. Now it was time to see if it paid off. The company rolled out new products, refined its sales and marketing strategies, and moved into automation. Convinced that the American economy was about to take off, U.A. Whitaker turned away the military and government contracts that had once supported the company to concentrate on consumer goods. It was all a calculated gamble. If nothing had changed in the economy, if Americans from Seattle to Savannah didn't rush to stores, it is possible that A-MP might have remained a small electrical parts supplier. But Whitaker and his top engineers were right: American industry boomed like it never had before, and A-MP was exactly where it wanted to be.

During the 1950s, the U.S. gross national product rose from $285 billion to $504 billion, while direct foreign investment, spurred by the postwar economic climate in Western Europe, rose from $11 billion to $32 billion.[2] A-MP itself reaped the rewards as sales shot from $5.5 million in 1950 to $21.6 million by 1955.[3] Momentum also carried A-MP overseas, which would prove to be one of the most important moves in the history of the company.

As expected, the domestic electronics industry exploded as demand for component parts (such as transistors and capacitors as well as the kind of product made by A-MP) paralleled the increased demand for end products such as appliances, TVs and computers. Sales of data processing equipment alone jumped from $25 million in 1953 to $1 billion by 1960.[4] The percentage of homes with TVs rose astronomically during the decade, from about 26 percent in 1950 to 90 percent in 1959. The share of homes with electric washers rose from 72 to 93 percent in the same period; refrigerators, from 86 to 98 percent; and vacuum cleaners, from 57 to 73 percent.[5] All these electrical appliances required terminals and connectors, and manufacturers needed high-speed, low-cost means of applying them.

All across the country, people were buying houses, stocking them with appliances, and driving to and from work in record numbers.

The Korean War: Mini-Boom

The consumer buying spree was helped along by another war, this time in Korea. The imprint of World War II rationing still was very much alive in the public's memory, and people

---

Shown in 1955, the A-MP Mobilab helped the sales force reach more people, more quickly and demonstrate the wide range of products.

wanted to squeeze in their shopping before access to goods was shut down again.[6] When America did enter the Korean War in 1950, the country once again primed its war machine, but this time not at the expense of the average consumer.

Communist North Korean troops under Kim Il Sung invaded South Korea on June 25 in an attempt to reunify the country, which had been arbitrarily divided at the 38th parallel in 1945. The invasion took the world by surprise, and North Korean troops quickly overran the capital city of Seoul. President Harry S. Truman implored U.S. citizens to unite their efforts to combat "communist imperialism." The United Nations declared North Korea the aggressor, and Truman immediately sent air and sea forces (under the Truman Doctrine) as part of an international coalition to defend South Korea.

He also called for a "mighty production effort" to rebuild American military might. Defense

---

In the 1950s, A-MP found a huge potential market in automobiles. Working closely with the manufacturers, the company developed a range of connectors and harnesses.

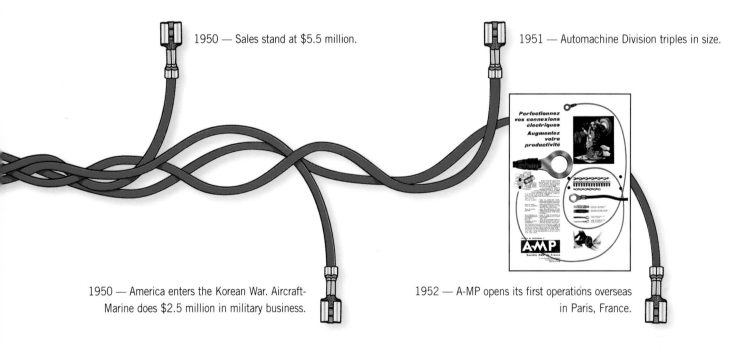

1950 — Sales stand at $5.5 million.

1951 — Automachine Division triples in size.

1950 — America enters the Korean War. Aircraft-Marine does $2.5 million in military business.

1952 — A-MP opens its first operations overseas in Paris, France.

spending skyrocketed from $13 billion in 1950 to $49 billion in 1953, creating another boom in the aircraft and related industries — which translated into about $2.5 million in business for A-MP between 1952 and 1956.[7]

Gordon Drane, A-MP's aircraft market manager at the time, said that Truman decreed every aircraft company was to subcontract to Boeing to produce as many B-29s as possible for Far East operations. And, luckily for A-MP, the plane's specifications did not change. "This meant that everybody then in the aircraft industry had to use preinsulated terminals made by A-MP and the requisite application tools."[8]

As the decade progressed, A-MP engineers were challenged to miniaturize, and cater to companies that wanted components.

The Early Fifties Lineup

But consumer goods really made the difference for A-MP and its future. The company was not content selling a product to satisfy a need. A-MP *created* the need for its products. Longtime employee Dottie Yingling, who served in a wide variety of capacities with many titles, remembered in a 1996 interview how A-MP opened consumer markets:

"One of the things I did at the time was to buy five electric stoves and take them back to the engineers. They took the back end off and they were horrified by what they saw as a harness because obviously those stoves were going to break down because they were wire wrapped and they were soldered and things of that type. So I challenged them to

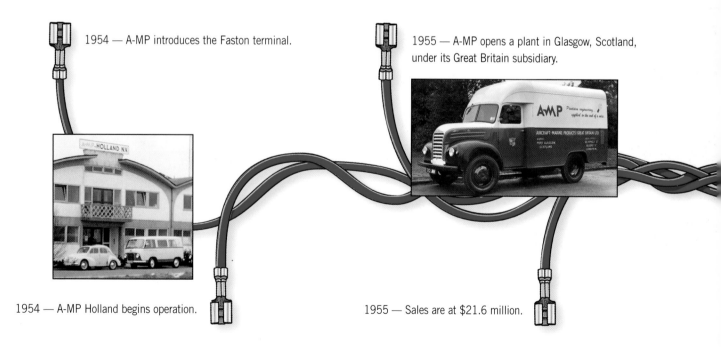

1954 — A-MP introduces the Faston terminal.

1955 — A-MP opens a plant in Glasgow, Scotland, under its Great Britain subsidiary.

1954 — A-MP Holland begins operation.

1955 — Sales are at $21.6 million.

come up with a good harness that would be cheap enough for consumer goods and demonstrate that we could just plug into it. They loved the assignment. So there were 32 companies that were making electric stoves at that time, and when I had this all ready, I sent it to all 32 salesmen who had one of those manufacturers. By the time the fellows had finished going in and talking to the 32 companies, they'd sold every one of them. Then refrigerators, freezers, you name it, all the kinds of things that are consumer goods."[9]

To some extent, A-MP's success during these years can be credited to a traditional company strength — research and design. In 1954, A-MP introduced the innovative FASTON terminal line, which was a combination receptacle/tab. It was destined to become one of the company's three biggest product lines (along with the AMPLIMITE and AMPMODU lines).

The FASTON terminal line was a classic A-MP design in several ways, but one that also marked a significant departure for the company. Like the family of terminals that preceded it, the FASTON terminal was essentially a simple piece of stamped metal crimped onto the end of a wire. The difference was that the FASTON was a disconnectable terminal — an assembly that consisted of two mating parts, a receptacle and a tab, that could be pushed together to form a tight, electrically sound connection

Above: In 1951, Aircraft-Marine Products moved its headquarters from Fourth Street to this building, a former roller rink at 2100 Paxton Street, just east of the city.

Below: The Junior Street plant in Glen Rock, Pennsylvania, as it looked in 1955.

which, unlike a standard terminal, could also be easily unplugged.

The efficiency of a FASTON electrical connection is achieved by the design. Two rolled springs create high-pressure contact over a broad area, while a springed dimple on the bot-

tom face locks the receptacle to the tab at the proper insertion depth. The design caught on immediately because of its high quality and low cost. It was a strong, reliable connection that could be applied rapidly in large quantity by automatic machines.

A-MP's first patent for the FASTON line was filed on December 29, 1953, in the name of legendary inventor Kemper "Crimper" Hammell. A second was filed the next day in the name of Angelo Lazzery.[10] The FASTON terminal would evolve into an entire line of products adapted for a wide range of applications. Former CEO Joe Brenner called the FASTON family one of the company's "giant steps."

Other products developed in the early 1950s reflected the trend toward increasingly complex wiring needs and the new premium on compact, space-saving design. For example, the taper pin, a self-locking terminal barely larger than the wire itself, was designed for wiring systems in confined spaces. It also was available in a flat tab style.

A patchcord programming system was introduced that greatly improved the speed and ease of installing and reconfiguring control circuits on automated machinery, test equipment and assembly processes. The system, which also found application in the first generations of computers, consisted of a patchboard with up to 1,632 contacts and patchcords — lengths of insulated wire with pointed terminals on each end.

The Automachine Division expanded steadily during this period, offering more automatic machines to customers as

no wonder it has swept the appliance industry!

AMP FASTON

Precision engineered AMP Faston Terminals have naturally gained wide acceptance throughout the appliance industry. Their extremely high speed of application and adaptability to subassembly production give an added "plus" to meet today's competitive production standards. AMP's exclusive triple spring action contact is extremely resistant to vibration and can be assembled on the production line with the assurance of a perfect electrical connection. Faston terminals are available in straight-on or flag types and in Brass, Tin Plate or Silver Plate finishes. Let an AMP representative ... Faston terminals ... ion picture.

AMP   Send today for your copy of out brochure AMP's Creative Approach to Better Wiring

RODUCTS, INC., 2100 Paxton Street, Harrisburg, Pa.
ODUCTS OF CANADA, LTD., 1764 Avenue Road, Toronto 12, Ontario, Canada
Reprinted from "Appliance Manufacturer" February 1955

the new generation of machines was developed and more terminals were made available in strip form. In 1951, the division's physical facilities more than tripled in size, from 15,000 square feet to 51,000 square feet. This expansion included major additions to the Harrisburg and Carlisle plants and the opening of two new plants in nearby Mount Joy and Shrewsbury.[11] In 1952, 330 new terminals were added to those available in strip form, bringing the total to 970, while 1,600 machines were installed in customer plants applying these terminals, a 50 percent increase over the previous year.[12]

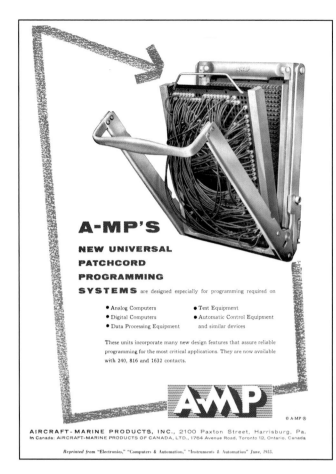

By 1956, AMP was producing four basic types of automatic machines: the original AMP-O-MATIC, capable of 3,000 terminations per hour; a larger, electric version called the AMP-O-ELECTRIC, at 4,000 terminations per hour; the Automatic Stripping Terminator, which both stripped wire and installed terminals; and finally the AMP-O-MATION Component Terminator, which installed various AMP products to electronic components, such as diodes, resistors and capacitors. The advertised machine speeds did not account for operator speed.

IBM and AMP de France

Though A-MP didn't necessarily set out to create a global corporation, the company crab-walked across the Atlantic in the early 1950s, and global expansion would follow naturally from there.

Left: In the early part of the decade, A-MP introduced a patchcord programming system, shown here in a 1955 advertisement.

Below: A-MP employees assembling the patchcord system.

A-MP made its first move in the international arena because of IBM. By the early 1950s, the two companies had developed a symbiotic relationship.[13] After World War II, IBM stepped up production of accounting machines and electric typewriters and began making a series of dramatic breakthroughs in computers, beginning with massive machines run on vacuum tubes and culminating in a fully transistorized computer by 1957.[14] By the end of the decade, IBM would control 75 percent of the U.S. computer market.[15]

A-MP engineers were there at each step, working closely with IBM to develop special products and application tooling to meet the company's expanding needs. For example, in 1951 A-MP developed a special piece of test apparatus that subjected IBM terminals to heat cycling in various atmospheres, such as ozone, ammonia

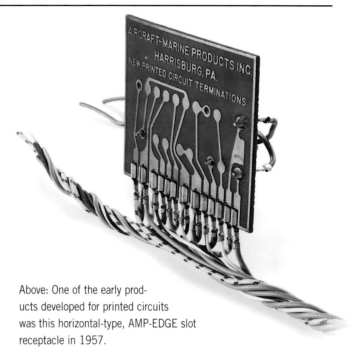

Above: One of the early products developed for printed circuits was this horizontal-type, AMP-EDGE slot receptacle in 1957.

Left: The AMP-O-ELECTRIC could terminate 4,000 wires per hour. A-MP's Automachine Division worked closely with IBM at first, then expanded to other industries.

and 100 percent humidity. A-MP engineers felt these conditions better represented those encountered by IBM machines than A-MP's standard salt spray test.[16]

The two companies' officers also kept in touch personally. In July 1950, IBM executives toured A-MP facilities in Harrisburg, Carlisle and Glen Rock, and left an invitation for Whitaker to tour the new IBM plant in Poughkeepsie, New York, as soon as it was finished.[17] In his letter of acceptance, Whitaker added, "We should like very much to have as many of your people as possible visit us at any time, as we feel such visits lead to mutual understanding and therefore better service on our part."[18]

The Automachine Division, still headed by Bill Pollock, developed particularly strong ties to IBM. In 1950, IBM accounted for 40 percent of the division's business, and though this share dropped to 25 percent the next year, the dollar value of IBM's business steadily increased. "This is regarded as a healthy sign," Pollock commented in the 1952 Annual Report, "for as the percentage for this one customer diminishes, similarly does the potential

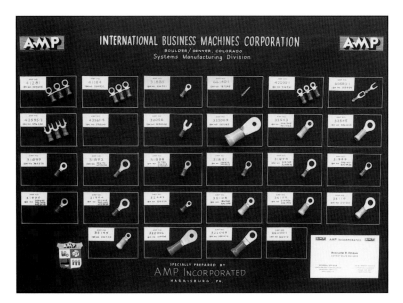

overseas confronted A-MP with a major business decision about how to meet those demands: Should it continue exporting the terminals, or license a European manufacturer to produce them? Or should it open its own facility abroad?[20] This last option was the most appealing, but it was a difficult risk to take for a young company without large reserves of capital.

In 1951, R.C. Campbell was sent to Paris to study the possibilities of opening a plant there. A graduate of Carnegie Tech in engineering and of the Georgetown School of Foreign Service, Campbell was uniquely qualified for the job and soon reported to patent attorney Marshall Holcombe that the situation looked favorable.

peril reduce, should for one reason or another this entire account be lost to us."[19]

Meanwhile, IBM's overseas operations were growing — a condition that would eventually pave the way for A-MP to establish a foothold in Europe. The increased demand for terminals

Above: A sample board showing some of the many terminals made by A-MP for IBM in the 1950s.

Below: In its early days, AMP de France was housed in an old perfume factory on the outskirts of Paris.

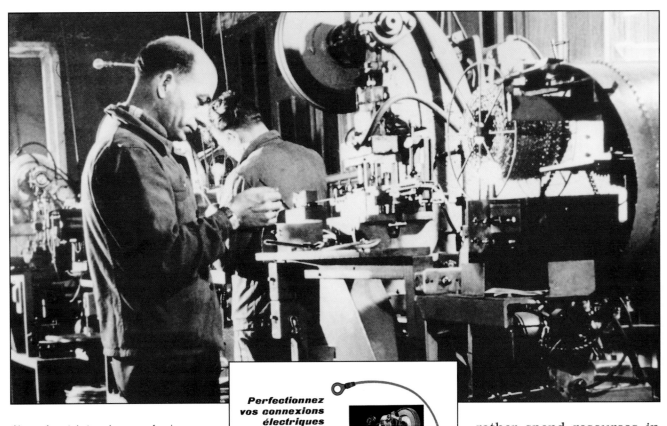

Above: A metal stamping press for ring tongue terminals in the early days of A-MP de France.

Right: A 1950s French advertisement for A-MP terminals that appeared soon after the opening of A-MP de France.

"It appears that a wholly owned subsidiary in France is eminently feasible at the present time. IBM has given us as much assurance as it possibly can that it will purchase from us in Europe for all their European plants. If we cannot supply them in Europe, they will be forced to manufacture themselves."[21]

Based on this recommendation, in November 1951 Whitaker wrote Cleve Fredricksen that "we have pretty much decided to go ahead with the Paris factory."[22] IBM could build terminals cheaper but would rather spend resources in other areas.

In February 1952, Bill Pollock was put in charge of setting up the French operation. A building was found near the River Seine on the outskirts of Paris, and equipment was shipped from Harrisburg in August. "We resurrected some old dies and machines and sent them over," recalled Ken Neijstrom, who headed Harrisburg production at the time.[23]

The building had been an old perfume factory, recalled Pollock. "I use the word factory loosely because it was about the size of a large house, period."[24] The original factory was on low ground near the river, and the basement was still rented to a man who made perfume — a combination that created some amusing scenes, recounted W. Gordon Drane, then director of Product Communication for A-MP.

The terminal production operation in 's-Hertogenbosch, Holland, in 1955. A-MP was welcomed in the country and used it as a base of expansion, eventually developing an engineering department and development lab there.

"When the Seine would flood, all these big green perfume bottles would be floating around the cellar and then would come up to the first floor where our presses were jacked up on blocks to keep them running. The press operators would be in hip boots, and these damned perfume bottles would be bobbing up the stairs."[25]

On August 25, 1952, IBM's first shipment of 800,000 terminals left the loading dock at AMP de France. Orders from IBM plants in Italy, Germany, Scotland and Holland followed the next month.[26]

As it turned out, AMP de France had no problem satisfying IBM's needs. Rather, as Campbell reported to Pollock in October 1952, the problem was finding more European customers, as "IBM's orders do not require our full capacity."[27]

To live up to its potential, AMP de France worked to cultivate accounts in other industries. The method was called AMPLIVERSAL, which was later applied to all of Europe.

AMPLIVERSAL was a "different direction to the OEM (Original Equipment Manufacturer) business," said Daniel Burnand, a sales manager for AMP de France.[28] Salesmen targeted highly profitable business in anything that wasn't an OEM, including automotive garages, contractors and the military, as well as some small OEMs. There was intense internal competition between sales divisions. Although the business started small, it would grow to 25 percent of AMP de France's business.

Holland and Great Britain

In the fall of 1954, Pollock, now head of A-MP's Foreign Trade Division, was sent overseas to assess the situation in France and scout locations for plants in Holland and England.

Negotiations with the Dutch went smoothly, and a site was selected in the town of 's-Hertogenbosch, in south-central Holland, 50 miles southeast of Amsterdam.[29] A subsidiary was established and production soon began under the direction of Burt Hendricks.[30]

The situation in England, on the other hand, was fraught with problems caused by the thicket of government agencies and regulations Pollock had to fight through to get approval for a plant. His nine-page memo to Whitaker on March 18, 1955, begins:

"This has perhaps been one of the most frustrating jobs I have ever undertaken in my life. As you well know, here in Great Britain there is no equivalent of Bureau Teppema or The Netherlands Industrial Institute, which were so helpful to us when we were going through this same business in Holland last fall. I have only written one previous report on activities for the simple reason that it has required the amount of time since my last report to accumulate the necessary information to try to put the pieces of this jigsaw puzzle together in a manner in which they would make sense."[31]

Pollock's long memo on the British situation ended on a note of cautious optimism. He saw the potential for a "very sizeable market" in Britain, but warned that it would take considerable investment in time and money to realize any profit.[32]

While A-MP's application for investment made its circuitous route through the Board of Trade, Pollock scouted factory sites and found more governmental hurdles. Because of living conditions, availability of skilled labor and proximity to the big airframe manufacturers, Pollock's first choice for a plant was the London area. The government, however, was seeking relief for the nation's out-of-work coal miners and shipbuilders and would only allow industrial development in economically depressed areas in Ireland, Scotland and Wales.

G. Earle Walker, far right, pictured with William Kramer, left, and Gordon Drane, middle, overhauled the sales effort in AMP de France.

Pollock initially was attracted to the Glasgow area by the presence of several other American firms there, including IBM, Burroughs and National Cash Register. When he actually visited the city, however, he was repelled by living conditions and finally selected a site 20 miles to the west in Port Glasgow, on the mouth of the Clyde. A-MP opened a plant there in 1955.

At the same time he was reporting on the British situation, Pollock found that the plants in Holland and France were still operating below capacity. He estimated the Dutch plant was capable of producing $20,000 in terminals per month, and the French plant, up to $60,000 per month. The combined sales of both plants, however, were only averaging $40,000 per month.

"It is these cold hard facts of life that make me feel very strongly that our single biggest problem in Europe is to produce sales, and I think that means that the sales force is certainly going to be have to be built up to provide to at least some degree the same hard-driving type of selling that has been largely responsible for the growth of the American company. I am certainly hopeful that during [Earle] Walker's visit here starting next week, he will be able to shape the beginnings of that sales force which we need so badly at this time."[33]

By the time Pollock returned to Europe in the fall of 1955, Walker had visited there, and after surveying the situation, Pollock predicted that the sales quotas Walker had set for 1956 — $500,000 for Holland and $800,000 for France — would be met.

In fact, the combined goal of $1.3 million in sales was reached by A-MP's European subsidiaries in 1956.[34]

A-MP's success in Europe mirrored its experience in America. The company found that it had to sell the concept of solderless terminals to new customers by educating them, and that the best way to beat the competition was to offer a better product, not necessarily a better price per piece.

R.C. Campbell, for example, discovered in the early 1950s that other European manufacturers were offering solderless terminals cheaper than A-MP, but customers could be won over when they compared the primitive European product to the highly evolved A-MP line.[35]

Tom Freedom encountered the same thing when he was sent to Japan in the late 1950s and had to contend with the cheap terminals being cranked out in garage shops. To dramatize just one aspect of an AMP terminal's superiority — its plating — Freedom would take an AMP terminal and an imitiation, bend them both back and forth several times, and then drop the pair into a beaker of nitric acid. "The cheap terminal would go up in a flash but the AMP terminal would sit there for minutes without giving up its plating," Freedom said.[36]

Earle Walker summarized the AMP quality vs. price philosophy in a 1953 memo:

"We arrived at our present position in the aircraft industry and, as a matter of fact, in the solderless terminal field, through the literal application of our slogan, 'Precision Engineering Applied to the End of a Wire.' We never have been price manufacturers in the sense that we have been lower in the initial cost and, as a matter of fact, we constantly have been able to face competition lower in price and overcome this competition either with a lower installed cost or a better engineered product, or both, and, of course, selling has had something to do with it."[37]

Pamcor, API and AMP Canada

Expansion in the Caribbean would almost parallel A-MP's movement into Europe. In May

The sales force in Great Britain used display vans, similar to their counterparts in the U.S. Shown is a 1956 A-MP Britain van.

1951, only six months before the decision was made to open a plant in Paris, Whitaker received a letter from the Puerto Rico Economic Development Administration trying to interest him in business opportunities on the island. The U.S. government had initiated "Operation Bootstrap," which was designed as an incentive to draw business to Puerto Rico. The letter stressed the availability of Puerto Rican labor and facilities for the subcontracting of defense work and the establishment of branch operations.[38] Further incentives included a tax break offered to mainland investors in Puerto Rico and the low cost of labor.

Whitaker urged the board to consider the possibility. Taking his advice, on October 23, 1952, the A-MP board approved the establishment of Pamcor, Inc., a wholly owned subsidiary for manufacture of A-MP products in Puerto Rico.[39] Four months later, American Pamcor, Inc., (API) was established in Valley Forge, Pennsylvania, to market the products manufactured by Pamcor.

As conceived, API would not compete directly with A-MP but would target OEMs who needed modest amounts of terminals, and after-market specialty accounts too small for the parent company to pursue.[40] AMPLIVERSAL in France was modeled after API.

Oliver Holmes from the A-MP Sales Division was put in charge of API and given some advice from his mentor, Earle Walker:

"Now, with any new company with limited capitalization, your first and most pressing sales problem is immediate business. Since your available cash is modest, then how to get that business at the least possible expense?

"A-MP had similar problems in its beginning, but yours are somewhat more acute. A-MP was fortunate in one respect: it did not have A-MP with which to compete. You do. As an important member of A-MP's sales department for over four years, you are aware, I presume, that I can either unleash the wolves or hold them back. After all, A-MP men have sold against lower prices and many other like factors for years and can continue to do so or they cease to be A-MP men. The wolves will be held in check, at least until you have had an opportunity to establish yourself."[41]

Walker pledged to help Holmes in whatever way he could, including providing names of possible sales reps and of customers A-MP had approached without success. But the message was clear: don't get into a price war with the parent company.[42]

API would subsequently become AMP Products Corporation, which included AMP Special Industries, AMP NETCON and the Distributor Marketing Division, all of which, in turn, were eventually absorbed into the parent company.[43]

In addition to its expansion into Puerto Rico and Europe, A-MP also opened a Canadian subsidiary, Aircraft-Marine Products of Canada, Ltd., in Toronto in November 1952, for sale and distribution of its products.

With an impressive portfolio of products, stability in the marketplace and overseas expansion, offers to buy Whitaker's company arrived regularly. AMP's files include a dozen such offers from the early 1950s alone. But Whitaker always replied to these offers promptly and succinctly: Aircraft-Marine Products was not for sale.

AIRCRAFT - MARINE PRODUCTS INC.

A-MP

Solderless Wiring Devices & Fixed Capacitors

HARRISBURG, PENNSYLVANIA   TELEPHONE: CEdar 4-0101

October 5, 1956

TO ALL EMPLOYEES:

We have realized for many years that our Company name "Aircraft-Marine Products, Inc." was no longer descriptive of the broad field of activity in which we are engaged.

Now we are supplying virtually every industry that produces electrical or electronic products. As you know, today A-MP products are used in all types of home appliances, electronic devices, business machines and computers, power and railroad equipment, automobiles and an endless variety of other products, as well as in aircraft, radar and shipbuilding.

Today action was approved to change the name of our Company to:

AMP INCORPORATED

You will recognize the advantages of this simpler name which retains the "AMP" by which we are best known.

U. A. Whitaker
President

In 1956, Whitaker alerted his employees that Aircraft-Marine Products, Inc., was changing its name to the more familiar AMP Incorporated.

CHAPTER FIVE

AMP GOES PUBLIC
1956–1959

"Insofar as possible, I think we should let others take over our old ideas, draw off as much profit in royalties as possible, and spend more time finding new horses to ride."

— Marshall Holcombe, 1956[1]

IN THE LATE 1950s, the modern incarnation of AMP was born. The national economy continued to expand, and Americans continued to buy more electronic goods — which relied on AMP products — than ever before. During these years, A-MP's leadership would look internally for change, steadily expanding its product line and recasting itself in an image that is more familiar to the world today.

The first step was the name. It was obvious by the middle of the decade that the company had outgrown Aircraft-Marine Products. A-MP's product line serviced a huge variety of industries, and the strict reliance on military/defense contracts was a thing of the past.

Since most people casually referred to the company as "AMP" anyway, a request was made for new possibilities. In an August 1956 memo to U.A. Whitaker, chief patent attorney Marshall Holcombe offered four possibilities: AMP Products Co., A-MP Products Co., AMP Corporation, and AMP, Inc.[2]

On October 5, 1956, AMP Incorporated was adopted as the new name.[3] At first, employees referred to the company as "aye emm pee," but the name frequently was confused with "A&P" the supermarket chain. The name was soon shortened to AMP.

Like many American businesses, AMP did very well in the last half of the 1950s. Sales stood at $21.6 million in 1955, rising to $32.3 million in 1956 and $36.1 million in 1957, a growth rate that exceeded the booming American economy. Whitaker continued to recognize the importance of foreign markets at a time when the domestic market was so strong. In 1957, AMP opened a wholly owned manufacturing subsidiary in Japan and in 1959 added companies in Italy and Australia, with Germany following in a few years.

Going Public

U.A. Whitaker had always been a forward-thinking manager who tried to anticipate trends in business, industry and technology. As such, he met regularly with his top people to discuss the future. These meetings began informally in the 1940s with a group consisting of himself, Cleve Fredricksen, George Ingalls (who would join AMP in 1957), Vern Carlson and Frank Wells, and later included G. Earle Walker, Bill Pollock, Bill Lange and others. Lange, who later became a cor-

AMP's corporate shield illustrating their varied product lines, circa 1956.

porate vice president, remembered that Whitaker was called "Mr. Ninevotes" because he could out-vote the others by nine to eight singlehandedly.[4]

As AMP matured, the name of the top level committee often changed — it was referred to as the Executive Committee and Steering Committee, among other titles — but it was composed of the same nucleus of managers.[5] In June 1954, the name was changed to the Planning Committee and it became the permanent forum for discussion of both immediate needs and long-range plans. At these meetings, Whitaker typically would encourage the members to look at the bigger picture.[6] His comments on the automotive wiring harness operation at the Mount Joy plant, recorded in the minutes of a 1959 meeting, are an example:

"Whitaker inquired of the possibility of putting an engineering team to work on this project alone to see if construction could be simplified and processes automated. Whitaker emphasized that this is actually another part of the basic problem of determining where this company should be five and 10 years from now, and then estimating engineering budgets and projects to meet these goals."[7]

In many ways, the future already had arrived. With investment opportunities opening up all over the world and a need for new space, the immediate requirement was capital. The members of the Planning Committee, including Whitaker, Cleve Fredricksen and George Ingalls, had been wrestling with available options for recapitalization, including a public stock offering.

But their decision to go public was not an easy one. For one thing, the corporate trend in the mid-1950s leaned towards mergers and acquisitions; more and more corporations were choosing this fast route to new technologies and products instead of the longer-term commitment to internal development and research. In fact, nearly all of the major firms that disappeared in the 1950s were absorbed by other companies in mergers.[8]

Historically, however, Whitaker had always diversified by reinvesting in his own company. For the first 10 years of its existence, AMP had paid no dividends on its stock. All the money was plowed back into the company, where it went for research, training and expansion. He had resisted offers to sell the company and so far had not chosen to offer stock publicly.

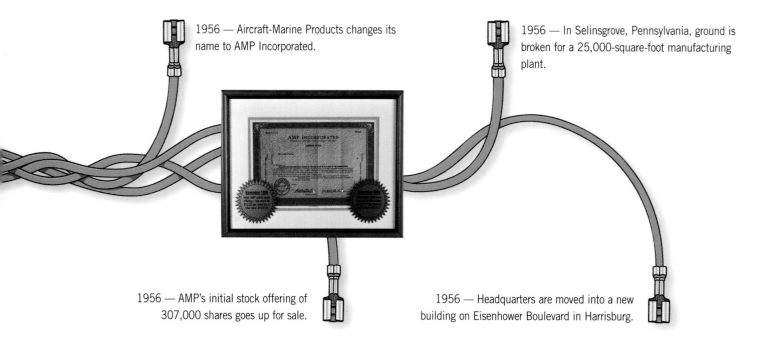

1956 — Aircraft-Marine Products changes its name to AMP Incorporated.

1956 — In Selinsgrove, Pennsylvania, ground is broken for a 25,000-square-foot manufacturing plant.

1956 — AMP's initial stock offering of 307,000 shares goes up for sale.

1956 — Headquarters are moved into a new building on Eisenhower Boulevard in Harrisburg.

Keith Funsten, far left, president of the New York Stock Exchange, gathers with AMP executives, from left, U.A. Whitaker, George Ingalls, Bill Pollock, and Cleve Fredricksen to celebrate AMP's initial listing on the exchange in 1959.

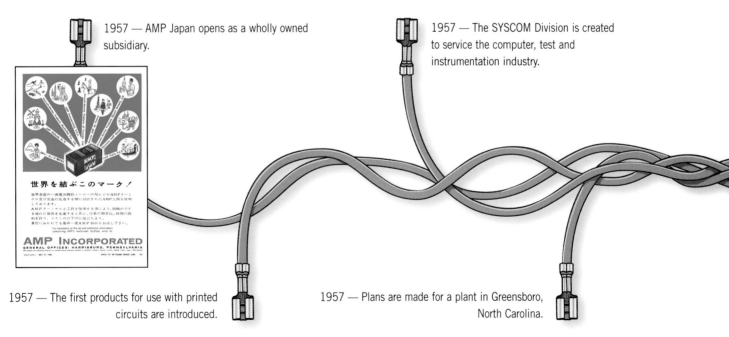

1957 — AMP Japan opens as a wholly owned subsidiary.

1957 — The SYSCOM Division is created to service the computer, test and instrumentation industry.

1957 — The first products for use with printed circuits are introduced.

1957 — Plans are made for a plant in Greensboro, North Carolina.

But these pressures finally came to a head in 1956, beginning with an April opportunity to sell the company. The New York investment banking firm Kidder, Peabody & Company approached Whitaker with an offer by Minnesota Mining and Manufacturing (3M) to acquire AMP. Whitaker listened. Preliminary talks revealed that 3M was willing to pay a generous $30 per share.[9]

The offer was declined, but the Planning Committee decided that a public stock offering, which included the company's employees, would be the best thing to do. In a September 1956 memo to the Operating Committee, vice president

AMP went public in 1956 with an initial offering of 307,700 shares.

and director of operations Bill Pollock announced the company's intentions.

"This action is the culmination of a long period of consideration, and the main points hoped to be achieved by such action are: (A) a wider distribution of equity in the Company, and (B) an opportunity for stock participation by employees."

He added that "the proposed stock offering would in no way alter the management and operation of the company as it presently exists."[10] Offering stock to employees gave workers a direct stake in how well the company performed. Higher efficiency and lower costs meant greater value for their stocks.

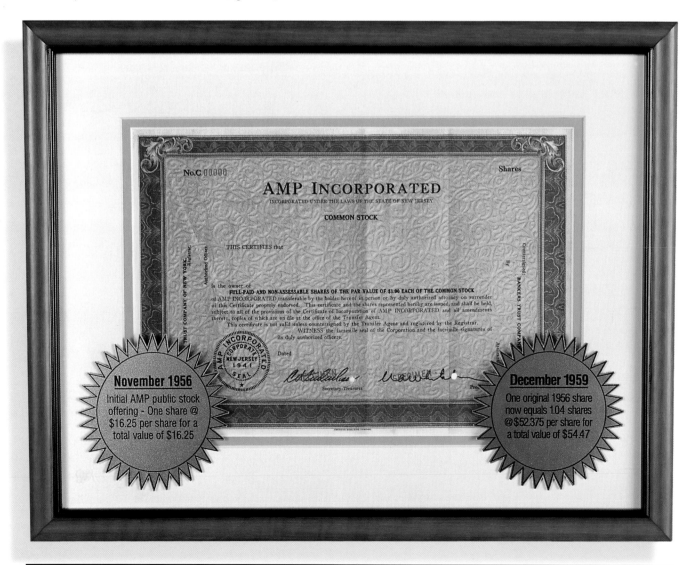

November 1956
Initial AMP public stock offering - One share @ $16.25 per share for a total value of $16.25

December 1959
One original 1956 share now equals 1.04 shares @ $52.375 per share for a total value of $54.47

The first 307,700 shares were publicly offered in November 1956 at $16.25 per share, which netted the company approximately $1.5 million. In addition to AMP itself, sellers included Whitaker and other original shareholders.

AMP employees were offered up to 50 shares at a lower price. Whitaker biographer William Cohn characterized the stock offering as a gamble.

"Whitaker determined that a decision to go public was in the best long-term interests of his stockholders, and although a number of years would pass before all the evidence was in, Whitaker's gamble proved to be a wise one. By the end of the 1960s, the company's growth rate had exceeded that of the 3M corporation."[11]

The Electronics Revolution

In the latter half of the 1950s, the electronics revolution had already begun to reshape domestic, industrial and military products, from guided missiles to computers to washing machines. RCA founder David Sarnoff discussed the growth of the industry for a 1956 article in *The New York Times*:

"As recently as 1946, electronics barely went beyond radio. It employed only about 250,000 people and sales were well below the $2 billion mark. In the past decade, however, employment has increased to 1.6 million, sales have soared to $11 billion, and electronics now ranks fifth among all manufacturing industries in the value of goods produced."[12]

AMP had managed to stay ahead of the competition and successfully ride the crest of America's new consumerism. But that didn't mean the company could rest on its successes. Electronics technology — including transistors and printed circuitry — was rapidly transforming the design of machines and appliances, creating

a demand for a new generation of electrical connectors. Nor was AMP the only player in the field; it faced fierce competition from old rivals Thomas & Betts and Burndy, both of which continued to market terminals similar to AMP's and develop new products for the electronics age.

Meanwhile, sales of AMP's bread-and-butter products — solderless terminals — were booming. According to the 1956 Annual Report, 90 percent of the business was in "terminals and related wiring devices."[13] The names of the top selling terminals were familiar: the vinyl insulated PIDG was the top seller in 1956, accounting for 57 percent of sales in the General Products Division, followed by the SOLISTRAND line (25 percent), the nylon PLASTI-GRIP (11.6 percent) and the DIAMOND GRIP (9.6 percent).[14]

AMP, as always, continued to "engineer the hell" out of its terminals, tinkering with established designs and spinning out variations. The FASTON terminal line is a classic example. Introduced in 1954, the terminal proved so popular and so adaptable that AMP engineers developed an entire family of FASTONS for everything from air conditioners to automobiles.

In 1956, the FASTON family grew to include the Budget Faston, for medium current applications, and the Junior Budget FASTON, which offered a cheaper and smaller alternative to the standard line. Also, FASTIN-FASTON connector

AMP FASTIN-FASTON connector used on the sealed beam headlamp harness of the 1959 Plymouth. The convenient FASTON family found a ready market in the automotive industry.

blocks simplified the manufacture of wiring harnesses. The unit, which was AMP's first connector, consisted of two plastic housings that mated to connect multiple wires terminated with Faston receptacles and tabs, respectively. The system simplified the connection of long, unwieldy harnesses by allowing them to be broken down into sub-assemblies. Chrysler Corporation was the first to apply FASTIN-FASTON connectors in its 1957 cars, with Ford later picking them up for the plug-in headlamps on its cars. Although it took longer to spread, the assembly also found customers overseas, where the FASTIN-FASTON housing was used extensively in Fiats. According to Vittorio Pozzi, who was in sales for AMP Italia in the late 1950s, the FASTIN-FASTON harness connectors accounted for about 35 percent of the subsidiary's sales as late as 1978.[15]

Moving New Products

AMP engineering was only one of the mix of ingredients that made the company successful. A large portion of the credit rested with the sales and marketing department and its approach to customer service. The process began with a meeting between the customer and the AMP sales engineer, ideally a salesman with an engineering degree. After listening to the customer's needs, the sales engineer would study his product and manufacturing process and come back with a recommendation about what kind of termination or connector package would best suit the operation. Once the package was sold, AMP would train the customer's employees in the use of the application tooling and then periodically send field engineers to make sure everything was working.[16]

An example of how the process worked is the case of AMP's development of a connector system for the York Corporation in the mid-1950s. York had been using a complex assembly consisting of a screw stud, bushings and a multiple washer stack to attach motor leads inside its compressors in room air conditioners. AMP, working with the Fusite Corporation, the main manufacturer of hermetically sealed terminals for the refrigerator industry, developed a system whereby a Fusite terminal could be connected with a FASTON receptacle and tab, eliminating 13 expensive metal parts.[17]

In 1958, the Sales Management Department, headed by G. Earle Walker, compiled a report of trends of the company's "Million Dollar Lines" and projected future trends. Although the top selling PIDG, SOLISTRAND and FASTON lines were expected to remain strong, other perennial favorites, like the PLASTI-GRIP and DIAMOND GRIP terminal lines, were declining.[18] Despite the

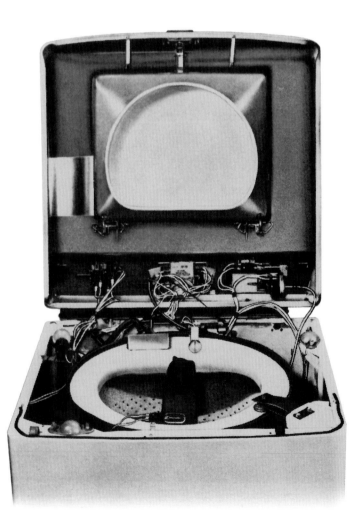

Consumer appliances like the home washing machine were a natural market. This washing machine used FASTON terminals with mating tabs and FASTIN-FASTON connectors for easy connect/disconnect.

A 1955 ad depicts the combination of AMP Faston tabs and receptacles and Fusite hermetically sealed terminals that helped the York Corporation simplify its air conditioner compressors.

continued success of its traditional terminals and all their updated variations, AMP was keenly aware that the electronics revolution might render its best sellers obsolete. Concern over this issue came from both within and without.

Bill Pollock, as far back as 1951, had noted the trend toward miniaturization in the circuitry of computers and aircraft and warned that "it is inevitable that eventually somebody is going to do an awful lot of this kind of business, and it would seem desirable if that somebody were AMP."[19]

In a 1956 memo to Whitaker about a long-standing PIDG patent infringement case against Burndy, patent attorney Marshall Holcombe concluded:

"Insofar as possible, I think we should let others take over our old ideas, draw off as much profit in royalties as possible, and spend more time finding new horses to ride. I have some feeling we may be growing fat trying to defend a status quo which we might better share with or leave in the hands of others (for a charge) while we make sure we don't wake up five years from now to find ourselves left behind."[20]

Signs of concern came from without as well. Soon after AMP went public, Whitaker began receiving letters from stockholders about AMP's position in the electronics revolution. One wrote:

"The other day a friend of mine, who is more or less an amateur in working on electrical things like the hi-fi for his house, commented to me that a more modern thing than AMP's solderless terminals are 'printed circuits' and that these should offer plenty of competition to AMP. I'm a lawyer and haven't any idea what a printed circuit is. However, I do consider I have some sophistication in selecting good investments, and it would help me to evaluate AMP better if you could inform me whether printed circuits offer any competition to AMP."[21]

Replying for Whitaker, Burt Hendricks acknowledged the growing use of printed circuits but explained that they had not replaced the kind of connectors AMP sold. He added:

"Interestingly enough, printed circuitry presents its own new termination problems which the product approach of this company is ideally equipped to handle. A printed circuit is merely a substitute for the wiring going into, say, a television set and still must be connected to other parts. Making such connections is more difficult with a printed circuit than it is with conventional wiring, and we have been doing considerable work in solving the new problems that are presented."[22]

AMP was indeed equipped to handle such changes in technology largely because of its continuing emphasis on RD&E, or research, development and engineering, expenditures for which averaged between 13 and 15 percent of sales.[23]

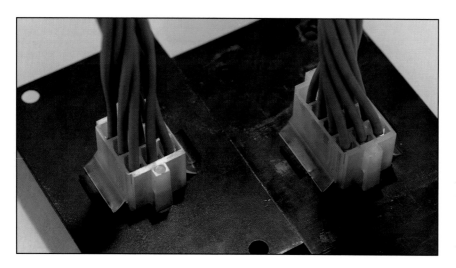

By the late 1950s, AMP-LOK connectors were available in a variety of configurations, including multiple-wire models for mounting to panels or printed circuit boards.

During the same period, the Capitron Division was busy developing products such as capacitors, power supplies and pulse networks for use in the aviation industry and in missiles. Established in August 1954 as the Chemicals and Dielectrics Division, Capitron was unprofitable for years because a lack of technical knowledge about materials hindered its growth. Although 1956 billings increased 50 percent over 1955, the best forecast was only that the division might soon break even.[27] The division was later sold to AMP employees.

AMP's Expanding Facilities

It is not surprising, then, that several products were ready in 1957 for use with printed circuits. The AMP-LOK snap-in connector with a leaf-type socket, originally designed for use in light-duty electronics, appliances and automobiles, was adapted for use with printed circuits. The AMP-EDGE and TIP-N-DIP were designed specifically for terminating wires or components to printed circuits. Later, the AMPMODU would become one of the company's strongest printed circuit board product lines.

In the late 1950s, AMP also began developing Multi-Aperture Devices (MAD) that used magnetic memory technology for storing and retrieving data in switches, electronic counters and computers. Bill Hudson, who would become CEO of AMP, started his tenure with the company working on the project. MAD devices consisted of tiny donut-shaped ferrite cores wrapped with fine copper wire. MAD technology was eventually replaced by integrated transistor circuitry in the 1960s.[24]

In 1957, AMP anticipated the needs of the new electronics age by creating its SYSCOM (Systems and Components) Division to develop programming systems for computers,[25] and the same year it also established a Technical Evaluation Department to review promising ideas developed by research engineering.[26]

The infusion of money from the public offering was put to good use immediately. By the mid-1950s, the company was operating several plants within a 50-mile radius of Harrisburg, including facilities in Glen Rock, Brodbecks, Seven Valleys, Tower City, Williamstown and Florin. General Products manager Blair Paules reported that the original Fourth Street plant in Harrisburg was pushed to the limit, operating a second and on occasion a third shift "against the complaint of neighbors," and "the crowded conditions were not conducive to the most efficient operations."[28]

To relieve the situation at Fourth Street, ground was broken in 1956 for a 25,000-square-foot, $500,000 plant in Selinsgrove to produce application tooling. Construction also began on two other new plants: one in Glen Rock and a facility for strip-form terminals in Carlisle.[29] In addition, major refurbishing was done to the original Junior Street facility in Glen Rock as well as to the older of two buildings in Brodbecks. The Seven Valleys plant was renovated to handle PIDG sleeve assembly and all of the company's plastic extrusion work.[30]

At the same time, expansion of executive offices was underway in Harrisburg. In August 1955, construction began on a three-story, $650,000 office building on Eisenhower Boulevard, not far from the old roller rink building at 2100

Paxton Street the company had occupied since 1951. Offices were moved to the new site in 1956.[31]

Despite the flurry of expansion in central Pennsylvania, management foresaw the need for a second base of operations and by 1956 had narrowed its search to North Carolina. In January 1957, Paules reported tentative plans for a 42,000-square-foot plant in Greensboro. "This has not reached the stages of reality but it would appear that some action may have to be taken during 1957 in order to provide additional facilities for our expanding terminal and tool business," he wrote.[32]

Managing all this growth required special attention. In November 1955, Leon Whipple, who

Founded in 1957, AMP Japan would provide the company with a launching pad into Asia in the coming decades.

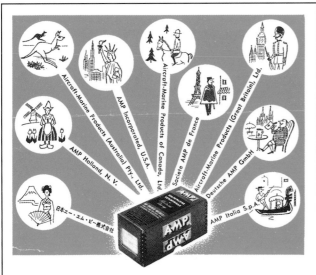

世界を結ぶこのマーク！

世界各国の一流電気機器メーカーの殆んどがAMPターミナル及び完全に圧着する様に設計されたAMP工具を使用しております。

AMPターミナルと工具を使用する事により、信頼のできる優れた製品を生産すると共に、作業の簡素化、時間の節約を計り、コストの引下げに役立ちます。

貴社におかれても是非一度AMP製品をお試し下さい。

For translation of this ad and additional information concerning AMP's world-wide facilities, write to:

AMP INCORPORATED

GENERAL OFFICES: HARRISBURG, PENNSYLVANIA

AMP products and engineering assistance are available through subsidiary companies in: Australia • Canada • England • France • Holland • Italy • Japan • West Germany

electronics • MAY 27, 1960   CIRCLE 101 ON READER SERVICE CARD   101

had worked with Whitaker at American Machine and Foundry and for A-MP as a site consultant in the 1940s, was hired as a full-time staff analyst. His broad assignment was to provide data that would "promote continued company growth and prosperity."[33] Whipple began with a statistical analysis of sales data from all the various divisions, which he presented in both historical context and future projection. With this information, he was able to give management an overview of company-wide issues based on more specific and quantitative information than had previously been compiled.

Whipple's job also included analyzing personnel. He studied the internal workings of divisions to make sure the right people were in the right jobs, that managers were delegating efficiently, and that those people ready for advancement were put on the right track. He developed a system to identify the "stars of the future" and to cultivate them as the next generation of leaders. His 1958 report to Whitaker begins: "The most significant change made at AMP during 1958 was the increased awareness of the need for developing an adequate supply of future leaders. Tools to be used in this development work include training, selection and organization planning."[34]

By the end of the decade, he was visiting all of AMP's domestic sites regularly, reporting back to Whitaker and the Planning Committee on matters of personnel, organization and customer relations.[35]

Personnel Changes

Whipple was not the only important personnel change during this time. As AMP grew in the fifties, several key people either moved into new positions or left their old ones. The changes reflected the long-standing trust and respect held between colleagues. Even more telling, it reflected a change in AMP's status from a "young" company to a more mature one.

George Ingalls, Whitaker's longtime friend and financial advisor, joined the company in July 1957 as vice president and controller. Ingalls and Whitaker had first met at AMF in the late 1930s. It was Ingalls who had put Cleve Fredricksen in touch with Whitaker, and all through

Aircraft-Marine's formative years, Ingalls had counseled Whitaker and Fredricksen on financial matters. When Ingalls retired as controller from AMF, a job was waiting for him at AMP.[36]

Ingalls brought to AMP the tighter financial structure and controls it would need in this crucial period of expanding resources, widening international presence, and the newly added responsibility that comes with being a public company. Whitaker saw Ingalls' arrival as a major step in AMP's transition from "a founding management to a professional management."[37]

To tighten the organization and control of its expanding foreign subsidiaries, AMP created the Foreign Trade Division in 1959 with Bill Lange as director. Lange had begun with AMP as a salesman in Cleveland in 1951 under Herman Haas, his neighbor and a sales manager for AMP. After working his way up through the sales ranks, Lange took over the IBM account after the legendary Bill Mavity retired in 1955. In 1958, with European operations growing fast, G. Earle Walker named Lange general manager for European operations. In 1959 Lange set up a new operation in Italy, AMP Italia, to supply Fiat with terminals.[38]

Also that year, Herman Haas was named director of domestic subsidiaries, which included Pamcor, API and AMP Canada. Finally, 1959 marked the end of Earle Walker's long and colorful career at AMP. F.E. "Bud" Howell replaced Walker in 1960. Howell inherited a professional sales force and would continue to encourage the work habits and ethics that would propel AMP into the coming global economy years before anyone thought of it in such terms. He adopted the belief that a manager is always seeking to train his own replacements. His philosophy was "don't hire people for what they do now. Hire them for what they will do in the future. You should hire anyone you feel could do your job better than what you are doing."[39]

For two decades, Walker had been the driving force behind AMP sales. Creative, energetic, flamboyant, eloquent — Walker was often controversial but never dull. During his tenure, he brought the sales department from an organization with a few sales reps carrying shoeboxes of terminals to a highly trained and organized sales force, closely integrated with research and engineering, that generated more than $50 million in sales per year.

Connectors

By the end of the decade, AMP delved into connectors, a move that would have tremendous impact on the future of the company. Although the move was daring, AMP was not ignorant of connector technology. The original patchcord programming system from the eraly 1950s had given AMP confidence in molding plastics, multi-pin connector technology and mating mechanics. In essence, the system was a large multi-pin connector.

Russ Knerr, who would head the New Product/Market Planning Division in 1988 after a 37-year career with AMP, boiled down the basic difference between terminals and connectors down into a few quick sentences:

"A terminal is a discrete device, which we stamped and formed. The connector, then, would take a number of terminals of maybe a different configuration and put them into a housing of many different types of configurations."[40]

Knerr's description seemed innocuous enough in hindsight, but at the time connectors were a hotly debated new

Top: Financier George Ingalls, a friend of Whitaker's, joined in 1957 and became president in 1962.

Left: G. Earle Walker built AMP's sales network before leaving in 1959.

AMP's national sales force meets in Harrisburg, Pennsylvania, for its first-ever sales meeting in 1950.

field. Whitaker aired his views at a July 1959 Planning Committee meeting, warning that despite the "increased volume of business in the connector field ... great care must be observed in calculating our return on investment in such business." Bill Pollock replied that although most of AMP's connector development had been done for the military, "we are fairly certain to have marketable commercial byproducts from this development."[41]

Pollock, of course, was right. And he was not the only one to support the move into connectors. John Eberle also was advocating the move, as well as a group of others. In fact, the decision to enter the connector field was one of the pivotal changes in AMP history. It marked a change in AMP's basic product focus. Up until the late 1950s, AMP was still essentially a terminal company, and although terminals had evolved into sophisticated devices, like the FASTON and the taper pin, they were still basically just stamped and formed pieces of metal attached to the end of individual wires. Bill Oakland, a lawyer and engineer who started with AMP in 1957 in corporate staff before moving into investor relations, remembered the period well:

"It was a critical point in the company's history because that's when we first introduced connectors for printed circuit boards, coaxial cables and multiple wires. We moved from being primarily terminals, which was a controversial issue. Do we stick with that because we're a leader, or is there a trend that it's going to be to more and more connectors? It looks like a seamless, obvious, no-brainer, but it was fiercely debated at the time."[42]

In 1959 and 1960, AMP's connector program only accounted for a small share of AMP's sales, but with high growth and profitability. In 1959, sales for connectors stood at $500,000 out of a total sales volume of $43.2 million. In 1960, connector sales grew to $750,000, while total sales had mushroomed to $53.9 million. However, the connector business would grow so fast that a separate division would be created in 1962, by which time connectors were accounting for 20 percent of all AMP sales.[43]

This system at Motorola, an AMP-designed and assembled manufacturing line, made TV repair easier by modularizing various functions, all of which became pluggable and field replacable through the AMP-MODU interconnection system.

CHAPTER SIX

CONNECTING WITH THE FUTURE
1960–1969

"I feel that the inventors or the engineers have to be permitted to make mistakes and to bring out products that maybe aren't going to be that successful because if you bring out ten new products and one of them is a barnburner, you've paid for all the others, and you can't tell at the beginning which one is going to be a barnburner."

— Leon Whipple, 1996[1]

THROUGHOUT the first 20 years of AMP's life, technology evolved at a relentless pace, and the company, securely partnered with some of the largest manufacturers in America, had always kept up with new innovations and products. AMP found that it could rely on existing product lines and overseas growth, allowing the company to devote an unusually high percentage of its budget and time to research and design. Of course, not every AMP invention was a success, but the ones that did succeed fueled the company's phenomenal double-digit growth.

During the 1960s, AMP's technological savvy can be described in a word: connectors. Only a few years old, connector sales went through the roof almost immediately. Nonetheless, the decision to aggressively pursue the connector market was not easy; AMP leadership knew it would be more expensive than anything it had ever undertaken. But miniaturization and modularization of components, triggered by the widespread use of transistors and printed circuits, were sweeping the high-tech industries. The introduction of the intergrated circuit in 1961 accelerated the trend. It was crucial that AMP respond. Fortunately, this was not difficult. AMP had made a name for itself through superior engineering, precisely the quality that would position it so well for the coming Information Age.

AMP Joins the *Fortune* 500

As in the previous decade, the 1960s was a time of steady and general prosperity for American business. The GNP rose from $658 billion to $977 billion between 1960 to 1970, while personal income rose 59 percent in the same period.[2] The decade also saw the birth of modern corporate giants. Some 200 companies passed the billion-dollar mark in sales by 1970, and five (AT&T, Prudential Insurance, Metropolitan Life Insurance, Standard Oil and IBM) reached that figure in net income alone.[3]

While not yet at $1 billion in sales, AMP saw its revenue increase dramatically, vaulting the company into the *Fortune* 500 in 1966 (AMP's 25th anniversary) for the first time. From 1960 to 1969, sales rose from $53.9 million to a record $211 million.[4] In 1967, however, AMP suffered a drop in earnings, from $15 million in 1966 to $14.1 million. Analysts said the drop reflected an anticipated fall-off in sales after the unusually fast growth.

These kinds of figures couldn't have been posted unless something momentous was happening in

The M-series connector was named for its military origins. The product signalled AMP's move into the pin-and-socket connector market.

By the late 1960s, an increasing number of AMP terminals were available in strip form on reels for automatic application with one of AMP's machines.

place, and consumers were quick to respond. Also, in hindsight, it was easy to spot the forerunners of the technologically explosive Information Age. As defined by business historian Alex Groner, the "knowledge industry" of the 1960s was "an uneven mixture of education, printed and electronic communication, computers, and various management and executive functions" that focused on the dissemination of information.[5]

Two multibillion-dollar companies — IBM and AT&T — were at the center of this technological revolution, and their advances had a ripple effect throughout the electronics industry. IBM's momentous decision in the early 1960s to concentrate on a new family of computers, the System 360, resulted in the development of hardware with 30,000 components per cubic foot, compared to 5,000 per cubic foot in the previous generation of computers.[6] The increasing complexity of electronic hardware, in turn, created the need for smaller and more sophisticated electrical connectors.

AMP's Connector Product Division

the industrial world. By this time, technological change was a way of life for American business. More advanced products were flooding the market-

The story of connectors at AMP is the story of a company taking what it did best — stamping

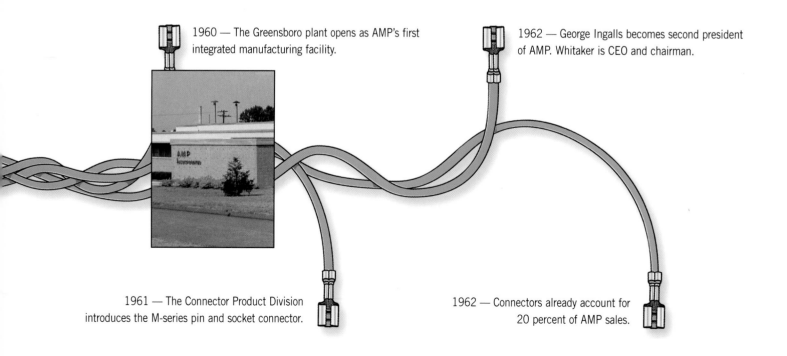

1960 — The Greensboro plant opens as AMP's first integrated manufacturing facility.

1962 — George Ingalls becomes second president of AMP. Whitaker is CEO and chairman.

1961 — The Connector Product Division introduces the M-series pin and socket connector.

1962 — Connectors already account for 20 percent of AMP sales.

and forming metal — and adapting that process to a completely new family of products.

In 1959, AMP established a Connector Products Department within its General Products Division. The move was prompted by a demand for connectors from U.A. Whitaker's least-preferred customer, the military. Boeing had approached AMP about developing a connector for the surface-to-air Bomarc missile. "Boeing engineers came in asking that AMP take a military contract. They were willing to pay for the development of the connector, but then it would be a military standard that could be manufactured by any number of companies," explained Joe Sweeney, a former systems engineer at North American Aviation who came to AMP in 1955.[7] He later became vice president of technology.

To the dismay of the Marketing Department, Whitaker declined Boeing's request, but his reasons were far-sighted, according to Sweeney.

"He knew you had to apply your engineering to build the future of the company. When you take a military contract, you, in effect, sell your engineering. They become the owners of the products. You may be a supplier, but they own the products because they own the drawings. You no longer are your own master."[8]

In fact, AMP's first connectors replicated existing military connectors made by Winchester and Continental in both size and configuration. However, the multiposition connectors being

Aerospace connectors, circa 1969, represented AMP's finest technology. Shown in the rear is the high-density, Subminiature D-series connector.

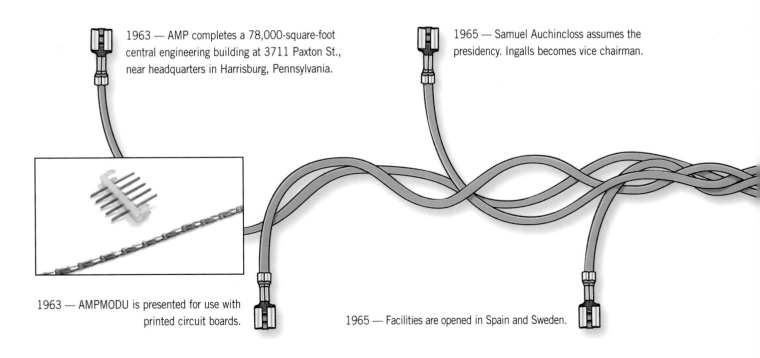

1963 — AMP completes a 78,000-square-foot central engineering building at 3711 Paxton St., near headquarters in Harrisburg, Pennsylvania.

1965 — Samuel Auchincloss assumes the presidency. Ingalls becomes vice chairman.

1963 — AMPMODU is presented for use with printed circuit boards.

1965 — Facilities are opened in Spain and Sweden.

used by the military in the 1950s were made from screw machine parts to which wires were soldered. This design carried all the disadvantages AMP had already engineered out of its original terminals: the labor costs, extra time and variability involved in soldering. Moreover, multiple-position connectors with their numerous tiny contacts required even more highly skilled soldering than single terminals.[9]

AMP committed itself to developing a solderless connector, which required a considerable investment in engineering and tooling. The crimped contacts themselves presented a formidable engineering problem. Homer Henschen, product manager for the original M-Series connector, began working on the project in November 1958. He spent most of 1959 developing a design for pins and sockets small enough to mate, providing reliable electrical connections in the confined space of a housing that held 50 to 100 contacts.[10]

One of the major challenges was to build dies precise enough to produce the tolerances required, recalled Henschen. The presses AMP used at the time for terminals like the PIDG were capable of tolerances of around three one-thousandths of an inch. To make the tiny pins and sockets in a multiple-position connector, tolerances of one-and-a-half one-thousandths of an inch were required. Such precision was easy to achieve with screw machine parts, but it demanded new, more sophisticated techniques in stamping and forming metal. As it turned out, AMP would have to upgrade its presses over the next decade, from the $35,000 models it was using on standard terminals to machines costing $250,000 and more.[11]

The development of connectors also would require advances in plating since the pin and socket design is a low-pressure connection that depends on highly conductive plating for its electrical reliability. Gold is ideal for such applications, and AMP had to develop economical ways of plating with this and other expensive materials. By 1960, X-rays were being used to measure plating thickness more precisely, and the production process had been reduced from three steps to one.[12]

The connector project also created the need for an expanded in-house Plastics Department, which involved a substantial investment in people

AMP engineer Homer Henschen explains electronic packaging at a 1969 aircraft/avionics workshop in Harrisburg.

and facilities.[13] The Plastics Department's engineering leader was Bill Narigan, who would become the divison manager of Plastics Products before rising to vice president of Quality. The department developed products for every division. In the long run, in-house plastic housing development saved money, but in the short run, Narigan reported that development and tooling raised initial costs.[14]

Whitaker must have foreseen many of these development costs, and they gave him pause. But one of his traits as a leader was a willingness to listen to key people and weigh their opinions when making important decisions. Two of the people he polled in 1960 about the connector market were Joe Brenner, at the management level, and Henschen, at the design level. "Part way into the development program of these formed-up, strip metal-style of contacts, I was called into his office. For those of us at the product level, that was sort of like being summoned by God," Henschen recalled.

"He said, 'What are you working on?' He already knew, of course, but I showed him what we were doing and some of the early samples, some of the stuff we were showing to customers and whatnot. His next question was, 'Who are you going to sell it to?' and I said that some of the early people who were expressing a great deal of interest were National Cash Register, Dayton and Cincinnati Milling Machine Company. And his last question was 'How many are you going to sell?' I didn't really know, but I took a big flying guess and said, over the next five years, maybe $5 to $10 million worth. As it turned out, I was a little low."[15]

Brenner, who would be named vice president in charge of Manufacturing in 1961, was convinced that AMP could develop a better product than the screw machine connectors being offered by competitors, and told Whitaker as much. "I

told him that we could beat them by stamping and strip-forming [connectors]. They couldn't do that better than we could; nobody could."[16]

This far into the design process of a promising new technology, Brenner began to push for connectors to be separated from the General Products Division. In 1961, a separate Connector Product Division was established. John Eberle was put in charge. Eberle was a tenacious, able manager. He had been shot down over the Mediterranean during World War II and held in a German POW camp, and his management style reflected this experience, according to Henschen. "He believed that when you're in a survival mode, you've got to depend on each other."[17]

Don Shoemaker worked closely with Eberle for 19 years in the Connector Product Division before retiring as vice president of the Connector and Component Group. "I kind of call him my mentor," Shoemaker said. "John was a great believer in letting people do their thing. Outline the job, let people know what is expected and then let them alone to do the job. He was great at knowing what was going on."[18] Eberle was also known for his ability to detect problems in the early stages and move swift-

Injection molding machines at the Loganville, Pennsylvania, plant produce plastic connector housings. AMP's entry into the connector market meant the company had to quickly develop expertise in plastics.

ly to correct them. In one instance from the early days of the Connector Division, an AMP director phoned Brenner to relay an off-hand complaint from a customer about some AMP equipment at an Indiana plant. Five hours later, Henschen was on a plane to Indiana.[19]

The M-Series Connector

When the first M-series connector came out, it contained flaws that engineers had to solve even as salesmen were busy selling. "Pins were popping out all over the place from those connectors," recalled Bill Hildebrand, a California-based salesman who sold the M-series to airplane companies and later advanced to marketing and advertising and sales promotion management.[20]

As the product quality steadily improved, AMP found a market in the military, but on its own terms. Because AMP had developed the product independently, it still owned the technology. And the military applications were just the beginning of what was to become a very successful product line, used extensively in computers, office equipment, test and instrumentation equipment, and even automatic pinsetting machines in bowling alleys.

One of the great advantages of the new connectors was their "pluggability." They could be easily plugged and unplugged without tools, allowing servicemen to repair, service or replace components. This feature was a distinct advantage in an age when electrical devices of all kinds were increasingly made up of multiple subassemblies and modular components. AMP contributed with lower installed cost, which enabled the user to individually and easily insert and extract contacts.

Though the M-series was the most important of the first generation of complex connectors, several other product lines also were consolidated under the Connector Division in 1961. Among these were a family of multiple-position connectors for printed circuits, including pin and socket types and AMP-LEAF and AMP EDGE connectors. Meanwhile, work continued on the M-series

family of products throughout the decade. In 1968 alone, 200 part numbers were added, including new housings, contacts and accessories.[21]

Another promising new connector field was created by the increasing use of coaxial cable and shielded wire in high frequency applications where background noise had to be eliminated. AMP's Coaxicon and Termashield family of products filled this need. Another product, the taper pin and receptacle system, already widely used in computers, also was included in the Connector Division in 1961, as was the newly expanded plastics operation.[22]

The multiple-position connector business, which began modestly with a fraction of AMP's total sales in 1959, accounted for 20 percent of AMP's sales by 1962.[23] Interestingly, by 1967 the military would account for a major percentage of AMP sales, despite Whitaker's misgivings. Sales of AMP products soared because of two pivotal events: the military buildup associated with the Vietnam War, and NASA's race to space.

Above: An early rack-and-panel M-series connector featured metal backshells.

Below: A high-density, subminiature version of the M series, with strip-form contacts, was introduced in 1967.

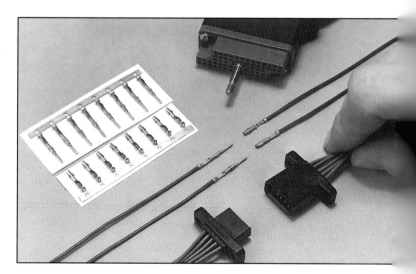

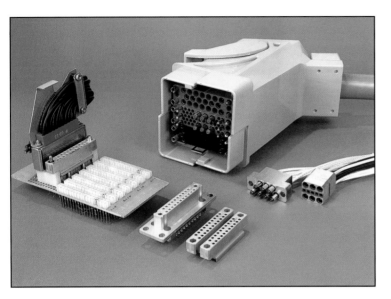

challenges and the personal contact the presidency gave him, but several factors made it necessary to relinquish the position. As AMP grew, it became important to focus on the company's long-term strategy and overall health, something that his new duties required. Furthermore, executives had earned the right to learn how to handle the rigors and responsibilities of the presidency. Also, Whitaker had been elected to the governing board of the MIT Corporation, which put more demands on his time.

On a personal level, Whitaker had suffered two heart attacks just a year before he relinquished the presidency, which is perhaps what eventually persuaded him to turn over the office

A Change in Leadership

In 1962, Whitaker handed over the presidency to longtime friend George Ingalls and became chairman of the board and chief executive officer. Whitaker had always relished the day-to-day

Above: By the late 1960s, AMP was producing a line of connectors for coaxial cable, which was increasingly common.

Below: From left, Whitaker, Ingalls and Auchincloss inspect the latest automatic application machine in 1967.

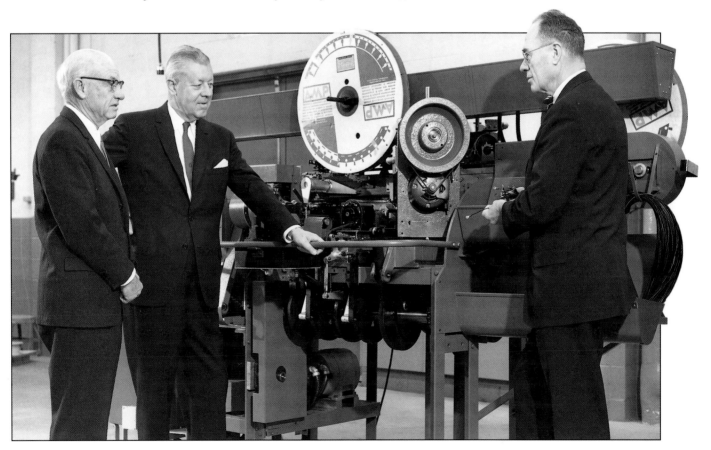

A Portrait of U.A. Whitaker

PHOTOGRAPHS OF Uncas Aeneas Whitaker can be misleading. He often appears unforgiving and unsmiling, when in fact he was sympathetic, generous and unassuming, as comfortable on the factory floor as in the boardroom.

An old story — possibly apocryphal — tells how an AMP employee was working on Whitaker's airplane at Harrisburg airport and got to talking with a man next to him, who was washing another plane. Unbeknownst to the first man, this was Whitaker. After they had talked a bit, Whitaker asked the man where he worked. He said, "I work at AMP, how about you?" Whitaker replied matter–of–factly, "So do I." Only later did the man realize he'd been talking to the founder of the company.[1]

Flying and sailing were two of Whitaker's passions. He took his first flying lesson in August 1935, while working for the Hoover Company in North Canton, Ohio, and was flying solo by Labor Day. The next year he bought half-ownership in a small commercial venture, McKinley Air Transport which he sold in 1948.[2]

A confirmed bachelor until his forties, his stock reply to why he hadn't married was, according to biographer William Cohn, "The cost of maintaining an airplane was just about the same as keeping a wife in good condition, and that a man could afford one or the other, but not both."[3]

In 1930, however, Whitaker met Helen Fisher on a blind date when they both worked at Hoover, she as an assistant manager in the stenographic department. Over the years, they kept in touch and dated, and on September 16, 1944, were married in a private ceremony in Baltimore. In 1946, the couple adopted the two teenage daughters of Whitaker's sister Minnie, who had died that year of cancer.[4]

Around the time he moved AMP to Harrisburg, Whitaker began sailing in earnest. His first boat was a 17½-foot ketch he kept at Red Bank, New Jersey. A succession of larger boats followed. By 1947, he was sailing a 38-foot Rhodes cutter. In 1949 he became a member of the exclusive New York City Yacht Club.[5]

Whitaker also enjoyed hunting and fishing and had a pistol range at his house.[6]

As a businessman, Whitaker had firm — some would say rigid — views about issues such as pricing, patents and licensing, and he was fiercely protective of products and technology developed by AMP.

As a manager, however, he was flexible and sympathetic.

"I would say he was a very calm, quiet type of an individual among people, in the meetings, and yet there was an internal drive. You could see it in his fingernails they were always bit to the quick!" said Bill Lange, who sold AMP products to IBM after salesman Bill Mavity and served as general manager of Europe in the late 1950s.[7] Homer Henschen remembered another side of Whitaker: "People were everything to him, everything." Henschen, who began with AMP as an engineer in 1956, recalled that he was always impressed by the extent to which Whitaker solicited and considered advice from his engineers and managers.[8]

Whitaker was known for trusting his employees and letting innovators be innovators. "He never told me to do anything," recalled Marshall Holcombe, who retired as vice president and general patent counsel. "Occasionally, he would say don't do something or do I really want to do that, but he never gave me any instructions to do anything. And he generally operated that way with the people that he saw a lot of. He didn't tell them to do anything. He turned them loose and they would run like hell in some direction. And as long as the direction was not too irrational, he let 'em go."[9]

Leon Whipple, an AMP veteran who first met Whitaker at American Machine and Foundry in the early 1940s, recalled: "He once told me that his dream would be to have a little plant of 200 employees where he would know every one of them by their first names and would know all about their families."[10]

Whitaker was a world class philanthropist who contributed — often anonymously — to a wide variety of causes. Himself the victim of recurring heart problems, he was committed to advancing the state of the art in biomedicine through funding of collaborative research among engineers, scientists and doctors. Upon his death in 1975, the Whitaker Foundation was established primarily to support biomedical research as an independent academic field.

Whitaker and his wife funded the Uncas A. and Helen F. Whitaker Building for the Life Sciences at his alma mater, MIT. He also endowed the M.D./Ph.D. program between Harvard and MIT and established the Health Sciences Fund in support of collaborative efforts between the faculties of Harvard Medical School and Boston University School of Medicine and Tufts University School of Medicine.

A lifelong concern of Whitaker's was the general welfare of AMP employees and their families in the Harrisburg area. Recognizing the contributions of the local people to AMP's success, he gave generously to community causes, especially those related to math and science education, but also to programs that helped disadvantaged residents to become self sufficient.[11]

A final word that inevitably surfaces in discussions of Whitaker's character is "integrity." "He was a man of extreme integrity," said Burt Hendricks, who spent 36 years at AMP, "and the AMP culture has always had that integrity."[12]

At a 1967 management luncheon, Whitaker gathered with his top executives. Pictured are (front row, from left) Bill Lange, Joe Brenner, Bernard Ryle, Ken Neijstrom, Blair Paules, Solon Rhode, Cleve Fredricksen, and Frank Wells; and (back row, left to right) Gerald Englehart, Leon Whipple, Bill Pollock, George Ingalls, U.A. Whitaker, Marshall Holcombe, Samuel Auchincloss, Bud Howell and Frank Kugel.

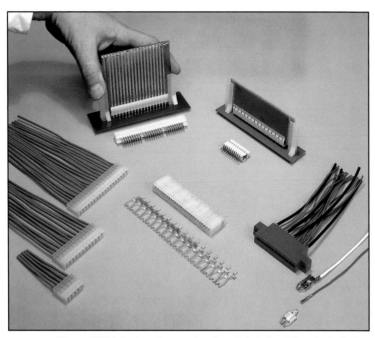

Above: AMP introduced connectors for printed circuit boards, including these circa 1968 products.

Below: The AMPMODU, a post and receptacle contact, was used in Motorola Quasar televisions' Works-in-a-Drawer. AMPMODU went on the become one of the company's three most successful product lines.

under Gen. Douglas MacArthur and had been awarded a Silver Star for his service.[24]

Some That Worked ... and Some That Didn't

AMP's new leaders continued Whitaker's strategy, pushing the company to develop new products. Not every new product would be a success. But Leon Whipple remarked that mistakes had to be expected:

"I feel that the inventors or the engineers have to be permitted to make mistakes and to bring out products that maybe aren't going to be that successful because if you bring out 10 new products and one of them is a barnburner, you've paid for all the others, and you can't tell at the beginning which one is going to be a barnburner."[25]

In 1963, AMP engineers began working on a new design for connecting printed circuit boards that was destined to become a worldwide standard and one of the most profitable product lines in AMP history.

The AMPMODU interconnection system consisted of units with rectangular (or square) posts mated to receptacles that could be used to connect circuit boards to other circuit boards or wires to circuit boards. The original product was invented by AMP engineer Bob Evans and labeled the MOD I. Several customers showed interest when it was first presented in 1963, but their immediate response was, "Can you make it smaller?"

Linn Lightner, AMPMODU's first product engineer, recalled that smaller versions followed "almost on the heels of the original."[26] A miniaturized version was introduced in 1964 that could connect "circuit boards, modules or memory planes, perpendicular to each other or stacked in parallel."[27]

AMPMODU's first two major customers were IBM and Collins Radio (a maker of aircraft radio equipment, since acquired by Rockwell International), but the product soon found a wide range of applications because of its size,

of CEO to Samuel S. Auchincloss, an AMP newcomer. Along with Ingalls, Auchincloss had been elected to AMP's board of directors in 1961. Previously a technical consultant to AMP, he would take over the office of president in 1965, and Ingalls would become vice chairman. Auchincloss would go on to become CEO in 1967, while Whitaker retained the title of chairman.

At the time of his election to AMP's board, Auchincloss was a vice president of Electronics, Inc., where he headed the Tracerlab Division. He previously had served as president of Cleveland Welding Corporation and Dewalt, Inc. In addition to his background in business and industry, Auchincloss brought an aristocratic presence and impressive personal credentials to AMP. A relative of Jackie Kennedy, he had been a member of the New York Stock Exchange before World War II and during the war served as a colonel reliability and adaptability.[28] Motorola, maker of the popular Quasar television, used AMPMODU connectors in its popular Works-in-a-Drawer system. Repair was an easy matter of sliding the drawer open and unplugging the separate components.

Also in 1963, AMP introduced a point-to-point wiring system called TERMI-POINT for the interconnection of wires in the back panels of computers and other electronic equipment. Typically for AMP, the system consisted of both terminal and application tooling, in this case, tiny clips applied by programmable machines or hand tools.

At first, the system appeared to have great marketing potential because it offered a labor-saving, more reliable method of attaching the thousands of small wires required in the growing complexity of electronic equipment. The product's most important selling point was the flexibility it offered the equipment maker: TERMI-POINT clips

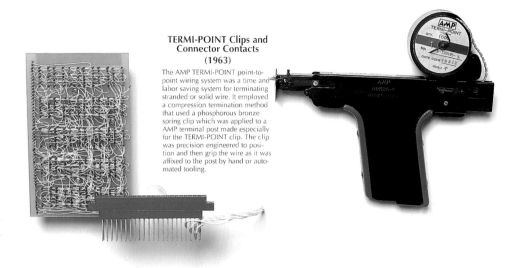

TERMI-POINT Clips and Connector Contacts (1963)

The AMP TERMI-POINT point-to-point wiring system was a time and labor saving system for terminating stranded or solid wire. It employed a compression termination method that used a phosphorous bronze spring clip which was applied to a AMP terminal post made especially for the TERMI-POINT clip. The clip was precision engineered to position and then grip the wire as it was affixed to the post by hand or automated tooling.

Above: The TERMI-POINT point-to-point wiring system was developed for the back panels of computers and electronic hardware.

Below: An AMP TERMI-POINT machine at a Hewlett-Packard plant wires panels for a computerized instrumentation system.

could be used on either stranded or solid wire and could be easily detached and reattached to reconfigure a wiring scheme.

But disappointing sales had not justified the initial enthusiasm, and in 1966 Ken Neijstrom suggested to the Planning Commission that the product line may have been "prematurely introduced to the field."[29] In 1968 the TERMI-POINT Division reported a net loss.[30]

The main problem with TERMI-POINT was competing against a simpler, cheaper system known as Wire-Wrap, developed by Gardner-Denver, which involved wrapping a stripped wire around a post. In the early days, the AMP system seemed to have an advantage because Wire-Wrap could only be used with solid wire. Such wire in the 1960s varied in quality, and as a result the TERMI-POINT clips were more reliable.[31]

However, wire technology improved and Wire-Wrap became the universal standard for point-to-point wiring. AMP continued to market the TERMI-POINT system through the 1970s, mainly for pre-wiring of back panels and backplanes for computer manufacturers, but the system never captured a significant share of the market and was eventually phased out.[32]

The MAD program of the sixties is another example of AMP's ability to determine where new technology could lead, and just as importantly, react accordingly. It was also another venture that did not pan out.

AMP had entered the field of magnetic logic in 1957 with the creation of its MAD (Multi-Aperture Device) program. By the early 1960s, MAD devices were used as memory units for storage and switching of digital and analog data in a wide range of applications. The advantage of these devices was they could store information safely and were "non-destructive," meaning they allowed repeated retrieval of data without destroying it.

The AMP-O-MATOR machine, shown in Germany, was one of AMP's most successful machines. It could cut a wire to length, move it into place, strip the insulation and terminate it.

Bill Hudson, who would go on to become CEO, worked on this project.

MAD memory units were used in satellites to secure data that was being lost upon re-entry through the Van Allen radiation belts. They also were used in the early sixties by General Railway Signal to replace the switching controls in its huge Toronto freight yard because the existing equipment was susceptible to lightning strikes. The New York Subway system relied on MAD technology for controlling its trains, and AMP Great Britain produced units for Imperial Chemical Industries for use in the "brain" that controlled automatic detonators for explosives.[33]

AMP's 1963 Annual Report was optimistic about the future of the MAD program: "AMP magnetic devices are steadily expanding in sales volume and product scope. ... As the need for capabilities beyond those of electro-mechanical devices increases, our reliable magnetic logic devices are finding rising uses in commercial controls and telemetry."[34]

It did not work out that way. By 1964, new technologies — notably, integrated transistor circuits and semiconductor memory — had emerged. For most applications, the new technologies were superior to MAD because they required less power and space.

Despite its initial enthusiasm and investment in MAD, AMP was prepared for this technological shift. In 1965, the company abandoned active development of new MAD products. A few select products survived and continued to be profitably produced by a small staff into the 1980s. The program, which was eventually sold, helped in the design of selective signalling, or paging, and TV switching equipment.

Joe Sweeney, who worked on the MAD project in the 1960s, cites this move as an example of AMP's understanding of "technology life cycles," crucial for a company so closely tied to the rapid changes occurring in the electronics industry.

"AMP made the decision well in advance to move out of the program, to shut down the investment in magnetic logic," Sweeney said. "A lot of people weren't too happy about it at the time, but it was a wise decision."[35]

It was part of the experimental culture that Whitaker had founded at AMP to recognize a failed project and let it go, noted Dimitry Grabbe, who started with AMP in 1971. Grabbe eventually became an AMP Fellow and director of Interconnection Electronic Research, and holds more than 450 U.S. and international patents. "Nobody succeeds on every try. In every research and development, you also have failures, and one of the things I found in my own experience the most difficult to do is kill something."[36]

Telephone and Utility Products

As technology expanded, AMP began to eye new markets and industries and in 1965 gained a foothold in the growing communications industry with the PICABOND connector. PICABOND connectors and application tools were used for splicing the tiny wires in telephone cables; AMP continued development of this product line throughout the latter half of the decade.

The opportunities for a connector company in this field were awesome and obvious. Telephone wires were run in pairs that had to be spliced to their counterparts to complete a circuit. A large telephone cable contained 6,000 wires, and a mile of such cable could require up to 63,000 individual wire connections.[37] Manual splicing, still widely practiced in the sixties, required a lineman to strip the wire ends with wire cutters, twist them together, and insulate them with a cotton sleeve.[38]

AMP's PICABOND system accomplished the same thing for telephone connections that original terminals had done for soldered connections: made the process simpler and faster while eliminating the variables. By the end of the decade, one lineman working with AMP tools could join up to 1,000 pairs of wire per day.

One of the patents for the PICABOND connector and splice system was filed on February 6, 1969, in the name of James Marley. He started with AMP as a senior development engineer in the Automachine Division in 1963 and rose quickly through the engineering ranks: from manager of the Automachine's engineering development program in 1965, to manager of the Terminal Products Division in 1966, to a group director in 1968. He would eventually become chairman of the board.[39] The basic concept of accomplishing insulation displacement with an open U terminal had been devel-

AMP's AMPACT tool allowed linemen to fire a wedge-shaped connector between conductors and achieve a tight, lasting connection. Shown is an on-line disconnect. These products show AMP's application in the power industry.

oped. Marley added increased functionality to the innovation.[40]

The AMPACT Connection System

The AMPACT connection system was another important product developed in the 1960s, this one for use by power utility companies. The gunpowder-activated cartridge in the tool applied wedge-type connectors, consisting of a wedge and

a C-shaped spring. One sharp rap with a line-man's hammer fired the tool, forcing the wedge between conductors, which in turn forced the spring 'C' outward, creating a gripping action — all in a fraction of a second. In development, the tool was designed with shells but had to be fine-tuned by drilling a hole in the bottom and putting in some powder and primer, explained Bill Broske, who started with AMP in 1943 as a engi-neer and retired in 1975.[41] Broske was a legend in his own right; his colleagues enjoyed relating tales of the huge explosions that often occurred in his basement lab at AMP, and the development of the AMPACT tool literally shook the company: "He was a thing unto himself," recalled Howard Peiffer, director of Metals Processing Technology and later vice president of technology, in the book, *The AMP Story: Right Connections.* "He would set off big charges that would lift desks and chairs. The safety officer once went down and told him to stop the explosions. He stopped for about a day."[42]

After its introduction in 1964, AMPACT caught on gradually with utility companies. Stockholders were informed of the product's potential.

"But here the challenge lies in taking a product family that is now fairly well set in design and continuing the relatively slow education process required in selling to a more conservative field, where most new concepts are cautiously phased into use. However, to date some 50 of the major

AMP opened a 42,000-square-foot facility in Greensboro, NC, in 1960. The plant was one of AMP's first integrated manufacturing sites.

utilities are in various stages of using or evaluating AMPACT products."[43]

By 1969, Dallas Power & Light reported, "Nearly one-half million applied connectors later, we feel that the AMPACT wedge and tap tool method, as developed by AMP Incorporated ... has definitely achieved cost savings while increasing system security and reliability." The company reported only 12 failures in 500,000 connections, and all but one were caused by operator error.[44]

Product Development and Marketing

The increasing number and complexity of products in the early 1960s created a small cri-sis in the field. Many AMP district sales engi-neers at the time were terminal experts who lacked the background in electronics needed to solve customers' new connector problems. Furthermore, electronic technology was chang-ing so rapidly that a sales engineer responsible for an area or for one large customer could not keep up with changes and relay them to Harrisburg, let alone cultivate new product ideas in the field.[45]

To address this problem, one of John Eberle's first moves as the head of the Connector Division in 1961 was to create the position of product manager. This specialist was responsible for the development, engineering and marketing of a product line and worked as a liaison between the customer, the district sales engineer and the engineering department to anticipate customers' needs and solve problems. If IBM experienced a problem with an AMP product or AMP application machine in its Poughkeepsie plant, for example, AMP's sales engineer could send for the product manager, who knew that particular product and its application better than anyone.

In 1964, Eberle's model for product managers was adopted by all manufacturing divisions, and a similar system was established in industrial sales. It was natural in a company that had been working with customers in the pre-production stages for more than 20 years. The approach — which would evolve into the concept of "early involvement" — greatly enhanced the company's ability to respond to problems, anticipate customer needs and develop new products to meet them.[46]

Also, in true Whitaker fashion, patent protection steamed ahead, with AMP lawyers fighting to protect the company in numerous lawsuits. John Hopkins, who retired as vice president in 1986 after 25 years, spent most of the sixties in the Patent Department with Marshall Holcombe and was frequently involved in patent-infringement suits. "Patent everything you can cover and aggressively protect regardless of who it is. We sued GM. We sued IBM. We sued other people, and we caused some flak. We sued some customers but at the end of the day, I think we enhanced our position."[47]

Domestic and Foreign Expansion

Throughout the late 1950s, AMP had been investigating a site for another base of domestic operations, a "second Harrisburg." At the outset, Whitaker limited the search by telling his site evaluator, Leon Whipple (who had helped locate AMP's first Pennsylvania headquarters in 1943), that it must be no more than 400 or 500 miles from Harrisburg. These parameters were not arbitrary.

"He told me, 'I don't want my executives in a single-engine Bonanza for more than two hours,'" Whipple said.[48] A pilot himself, Whitaker had established the AMP AIR transportation department in 1952 to fly AMP executives and engineers, a service that became increasingly important as the company expanded.[49]

In 1965, AMP had expanded its Eisenhower Boulevard headquarters in Harrisburg to more than 100,000 square feet.

Raleigh as the first sites for its new domestic hub.

The first factory, a 42,000-square-foot facility in Greensboro, opened in 1960. It produced strip-form terminals and splices in an integrated manufacturing process, from stamping to plating, in one building. A second, 10,000-square-foot plant in Cary (near Raleigh) was opened the same year for production of programming systems for the SYSCOM Division.[50]

These two facilities were the beginning of what would become AMP's sec-

Above: AMP's second plant near Tokyo was completed in 1969, signalling AMP Japan's increasing importance to the company.

Right: AMP de France's second site, shown in 1968, was located in Pontoise, near Paris.

Below: AMP Great Britain in the 1960s was headquartered in Terminal House, Stanmore, in the London area.

Northcentral North Carolina fell within Whitaker's two-hour radius, and after scouting the labor and real estate situation there, the company chose Greensboro and

ond major base of operations in the United States. In the early sixties, AMP also opened a tool and die plant in Clearwater, Florida, that would later become a development lab.[51] These moves were the embodiment of a policy Whitaker had always believed crucial to the company's security — decentralization.

Which is not to say the headquarters were neglected. Although AMP had been headquartered in Harrisburg since the forties, it had moved around the city as more space was needed. From the original Fourth Street plant, to the old roller rink at 2100 Paxton Street, AMP settled in a new building on Eisenhower Boulevard in 1956.

But even that was not enough as the company expanded, and the Planning Committee looked into buying more land around the headquarters building. In May 1960, the company purchased 45 acres on Paxton Street in Harrisburg,[52] and by 1963, AMP completed a 78,000-square-foot engineering building that included test laboratories and model shops.[53] A second Paxton Street engineering building, nearly twice that size (155,000 square feet), was completed in 1966, next to the first.[54]

While AMP grew rapidly at home, the company assumed its place as a global competitor — although "global" had not yet been coined as a business term. A sales subsidiary in Mexico City, AMP de Mexico, was opened in 1960. Although sales were modest in the beginning (Bill Lange, vice president of the International Division, characterized 1961 projections of $250,000 as "better than expected")[55], AMP's presence in Mexico initiated further expansion south of the border, which eventually reached into Argentina and Brazil.

New facilities in Spain and Sweden also were opened in the 1960s. In 1965, a manufacturing subsidiary, AMP Espanola, was opened in Barcelona, Spain; and in 1967, Svenska AMP A B was established in Stockholm.[56]

By the end of the decade, AMP had three North American subsidiaries (Canada, Mexico and American Pamcor in Valley Forge, Pennsylvania); seven European subsidiaries (France, Holland, Great Britain, Italy, Germany, Spain and Sweden); as well as subsidiaries in Japan and Australia. There was also the PAMCOR manufacturing facility in Puerto Rico.

Every area that AMP expanded into required a detailed knowledge of the local culture as well as some memorable legal battles with local competitors over patent infringement. Richard Stuart-Prince, manager of international patent and legal, travelled a great deal for AMP helping to set up new subsidiaries and fight patent battles. "In every country, one was faced with a new legal system and new requirements for shareholding, directors, nationality of directors and so on. In some countries, you have to have a majority of local nationals. In some countries, it doesn't matter. There were changes in almost every jurisdiction."[57]

AMP founded a subsidiary in Germany in 1959 under Bill Lange. Shown are the AMP Deutschland headquarters in Langen in 1968.

AMP executives inspect AMP equipment at the advanced tooling lab with a Xerox official in the early 1970s. Pictured, clockwise, are: Joe Brenner, president; Bud Howell, vice president sales and marketing; a Xerox executive; Sel Friedlander, market manager; John Eberle, vice president; Bernie Britt, product engineer; and Rudy Gassner, sales engineer.

CHAPTER SEVEN

ON TOP OF THE WORLD

1970–1980

*"No matter how much you miniaturize, eventually that miniaturization
ends up lighting a light or ringing a bell or running a motor, or doing some
kind of work — and when you transfer from the tiny ¹/₈ of a square inch
circuit to something that does something, we're going to be there."*

— Sam Auchincloss, 1981[1]

THE EARLY SEVENTIES were less than stellar years for most American businesses, particularly when compared to the previous two decades. Between the bitter crunch of a recession and an OPEC oil embargo that left many Americans running on empty, the decade finally signaled an end to America's postwar industrial dominance. For the first time since the war was over, foreign competition was making serious enough inroads into American markets to hurt domestic corporations. Radios from Japan and West Germany became more and more common, and Japanese cars began to arrive by the shipload. To compound this, President Richard Milhouse Nixon resigned his office, and the nation was still reeling from the Vietnam War.

But AMP remained seemingly untouched by the "malaise," as President Jimmy Carter would describe it, that seemed to have overcome the nation. The company spent the decade reaping huge rewards from its strategies of involving itself in the design phase of customers' products, and investing in more sophisticated automated application machinery to install the connectors developed for these products.

Perhaps even more important, while foreign manufacturers were giving American OEMs a run for the money, AMP also was supplying those companies with their connectors! AMP had quietly gone global before "globalization" was fashionable, even opening plants in the notoriously closed country of Japan. In doing so, AMP insulated itself to some extent against the trauma of trade deficits that would eventually rock the U.S. economy. From 1970 on, the international divisions of the company would consistently perform until more than half of AMP's revenues would come from overseas. By the end of the decade AMP would reach the $1 billion mark in sales.

But the middle of the decade was scarred when U.A. Whitaker died in 1975.

Leadership Changes

Key changes in the early 1970s established the brain trust that would lead AMP through the decade. Though Whitaker retained the chairmanship until his death, two significant players stepped down or cut back their activities early in the decade.

At the June 23, 1971, meeting of the board, Joseph Brenner was elected president to replace

---

The control board of the 1976 Magic Chef microwave oven plugged into an AMP printed circuit edge connector.

S.S. Auchincloss, who retained the title of CEO and would continue as vice chairman on "a less active basis."[2] One year later, Auchincloss would also pass his CEO title to Brenner.

Brenner, a Carlisle, Pennsylvania, native with a bachelor's degree from Dickinson College and an MBA from Harvard, had begun with AMP in 1947 in the Automachine Division and ascended through the manufacturing side of the operation. He was named head of the Automachine Division in 1955, vice president of the Manufacturing Division in 1961, and corporate vice president, Manufacturing, in 1967.

At the same meeting, Cleve Fredricksen, who had been with AMP since its inception and risen by 1969 to chief financial officer and corporate vice president, was appointed chairman of the newly created Finance Committee.

Bill Lange was elected senior vice president, Merchandising, and W. B. Conner was appointed

From left, Joe Brenner, U.A. Whitaker and Samuel Auchincloss inspect a 1971 AMP-O-MATOR machine. The machine was one of AMP's most important automatic application machines provided to customers.

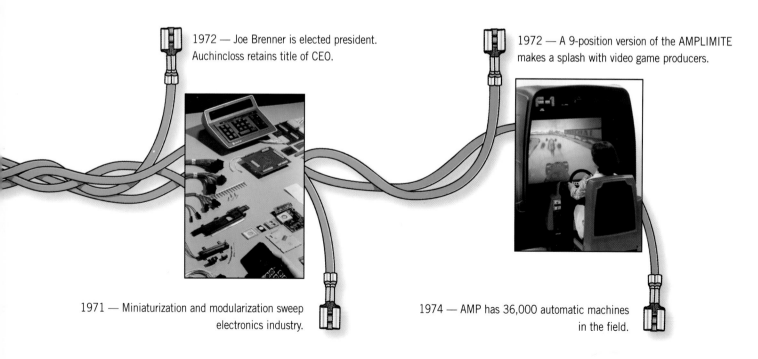

1972 — Joe Brenner is elected president. Auchincloss retains title of CEO.

1972 — A 9-position version of the AMPLIMITE makes a splash with video game producers.

1971 — Miniaturization and modularization sweep electronics industry.

1974 — AMP has 36,000 automatic machines in the field.

vice president of the Industrial Sales Division. Finally, treasurer Walter Raab was named corporate vice president. A Philadelphia-area native and CPA with a degree from the Wharton School of Business, Raab had ascended through the financial side of the company. He began with American Pamcor in 1953 and moved to Harrisburg three years later. Raab was named treasurer in 1967 and would eventually become CEO.

Longtime Whitaker friend and adviser George Ingalls retired from the board in 1971 because of ill health. He had counseled Whitaker from the earliest days of the company and was the key architect of AMP's financial structure. After officially joining the company in 1956, Ingalls held the successive titles of vice president-controller (1957), executive vice president (1960), president (1962) and vice chairman of the board (1965). He died in August 1972.

Staying Ahead of the Game

By 1970, "connector" had replaced "terminal" as the generic term for AMP products, and the company was commonly referred to in the press as "the world's leading manufacturer of connection devices."[3] AMP had built a healthy lead in market share over its two old rivals — Thomas & Betts and Burndy — and also was well ahead of the competition, including Amphenol, Berg Electronics and Molex.

The trend of the 1960s — miniaturization, modularization and circuit integration — accelerated in the early 1970s with the introduction of semiconductor technology that put

Input/output connectors with miniature contacts offered in 1971.

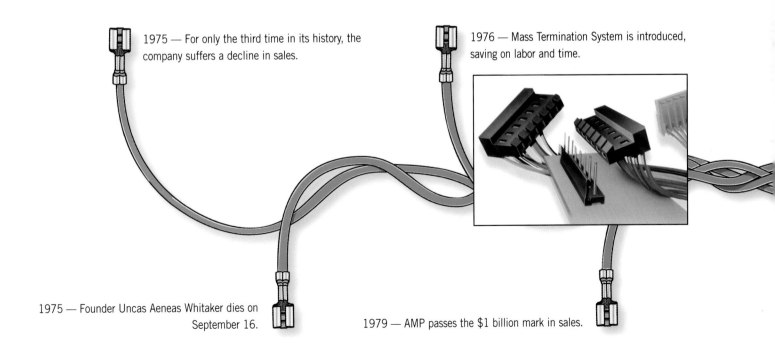

1975 — For only the third time in its history, the company suffers a decline in sales.

1976 — Mass Termination System is introduced, saving on labor and time.

1975 — Founder Uncas Aeneas Whitaker dies on September 16.

1979 — AMP passes the $1 billion mark in sales.

"*No matter how much you miniaturize, eventually that miniaturization ends up lighting a light or ringing a bell or running a motor, or doing some kind of work — and when you transfer from the tiny 1/8 of a square inch circuit to something that does something, we're going to be there.*"[5]

Economation

The term "Economation" (derived from ECONOmy and autoMATION) first appeared in AMP's 1969 Annual Report and was featured in all company literature of the 1970s. It was a new name for an old concept: the idea that AMP could provide customers with earlier involvement in their design process and the high-speed, automated machines to apply the resulting products.

The electronics industry of the early 1970s was ripe for a concept like Economation. Consumers' appetite for electronics increased in the early part of

Left: Taken from the 1973 Annual Report, calculators are shown with the miniaturized AMP products that went into them. Miniaturization and modularization changed AMP's product design focus.

Below: The 1973 Stromberg-Carlson telephone included AMP terminals, receptacle connectors, pins and strain-relief clips.

previously bulky and expensive products like calculators within reach of the average consumer. As technology went forward in leaps and bounds, AMP's products became steadily more complex. The company that had been founded on simple crimping had moved into ceramics, plating, plastics, semiconductor technology and other demanding fields. As Howard Peiffer, vice president of Global Technology, remarked in a 1997 interview, "The connector business is a very complex one. It involves mechanical engineering. It involves industrial engineering. It involves chemical engineering. All the engineering functions plus physics, metallurgy, materials science and the like."[4]

Some stockholders worried that the rapid pace of change would render AMP's products obsolete. But CEO Samuel Auchincloss scoffed at the notion in 1971, making what would prove to be a perceptive comment:

A telephone lineman uses an AMP PICABOND tool and splices to splice telephone cable. With PICABOND, the company gained access into the lucrative communication field.

the decade, making high volume production a must for OEMs. The market for household electronic products (TVs, stereos, calculators, etc.) alone nearly doubled between 1971 and 1973, from about 15 percent of the total market to more than 27 percent. This increase, in turn, created a shortage of parts.[6]

An article in the December 1973 issue of *Electronic Design News* analyzed the reasons behind these shortages: "The primary reason we are currently in the midst of severe product scarcity is quite simple: the magnitude of the consumer business and the short time it took to reach this level surprised nearly everyone."[7]

The high volumes at which new products were being produced, coupled with the rising costs of labor, made automated application machines a financial necessity for the OEMs at the heart of AMP's business. *Electronic Design News* studied the new generation of products being supplied to such manufacturers and concluded that "what these devices reflect are a blend of low cost, high reliability and the ability to be produced in tremendous quantities."[8]

The product/application tool approach extended to virtually all AMP markets. For example, the TERMI-POINT system was used to pre-wire connector junction systems for military aircraft and to wire back panels of computers. AMP high-volume lead-making machines were used by auto-

motive manufacturers for assembling wire harnesses. The PICABOND tool and splice were used to make the thousands of connections within a large telephone cable — the list goes on and on.

The numbers confirm the success of Economation as a marketing strategy: By the end of 1974, there were 36,000 AMP automatic machines in the field (the next nearest competitor had 5,000), and AMP held approximately one-half of the worldwide market share for machine-applied connectors and terminals.[9] Only four years later, two-thirds of AMP products were machine-applied, and the company had 45,000 leased machines in the field. As one industry analyst put it, "[No one] comes close to AMP in terms of automated tooling for high-volume connector use."[10]

Technical Advances

Economation gained added potential in "mass termination," a new method for terminating a number of wires simultaneously.[11] Known as MTS (Mass Termination System) when it was introduced in 1976, the label was changed to MTA (Mass Termination Assembly) in 1978.

MTA was made possible by "insulation displacement," a process by which wires are terminated to slotted contacts in mass, without pre-stripping the insulation. The process was introduced in the mid-1970s and radically cut application time.

> *"The technique eliminates the need for pre-stripping the conductors. Wires are simply positioned into the terminating area of the connector. Application tooling then pushes the wire into the slot to the proper depth. During the process, the slot displaces the wire insulation, and conductor deformation displaces oxides and other contaminants, producing a clean metal-to-metal surface for low electrical resistance."[12]*

A manufacturing process called "internesting," also developed in the 1970s, helped AMP reduce the costs of high volume parts by eliminating waste in the stamping of parts from strips of metal.

The AMP-O-MATOR, which was developed in the late 1950s in the Automachine Division, led the way as the company's premier automatic application system. The popular machine, capable of producing thousands of terminated wires per hour, combined the best technologies of the day. It was capable of cutting a wire to length, moving the length into place, stripping the insulation, and terminating it.

Above: Mass Termination Assembly products used one efficient motion to terminate a wire and insert it into its connector housing by displacing its insulation.

Below right: By 1978, more than two dozen AMP products were being produced with the Mass Termination System process, reducing customer labor costs by as much as 90 percent.

AMPLIMITE

AMPLIMITE connectors, the final jewel, along with the FASTON line and AMPMODU products, was added to the company's triple crown of product lines in the early seventies. Like the M-Series connector, AMPLIMITE connectors evolved from a military product to become the biggest selling connector type in the world. But commercial success in this case could never have occurred without a fortuitous licensing deal with ITT Cannon.

AMPLIMITE is AMP's version of a connector generically known as the "Subminiature D," first developed by ITT Cannon for military aerospace applications in the early 1960s. In 1967, AMP had begun work on its own versions of the Subminiature D, including a high-density model (with 44 contacts, compared to the standard 25) as well as a copy of ITT Cannon's standard model. Patent infringement was not an issue because military contracts allowed any manufacturer to supply a product that met its specifications, or "mil spec" in the trade. (It was this very contract structure that made military work unappealing to AMP.)

The early military versions of the Subminiature D consisted of screw machine contacts locked in place with metal spring clips. In 1971, AMP modified ITT Cannon's original design by using stamped and formed contacts with Cannon's plastic retention design, thus creating a product that could be produced and applied by automatic machines in high volume at low cost.

"Coming out with that commercial version brought us face to face with a dilemma," said Dave Rundle, AMPLIMITE product manager in the mid-1970s. "Then, the patent issues loomed."[13]

AMP had first inquired about a license to produce and sell its version of ITT Cannon's design in 1968, but serious discussions did not begin until October 1970, when the commercial version was in development.[14]

In response to a request for information from AMP's patent department, ITT Cannon originally offered its standard, non-exclusive licensing agreement, which called for a 5 percent royalty per connector sale. AMP balked at this arrangement because, aside from being costly, it was unwieldy. The licensing fee was based on the sale of a complete connector, whereas AMP frequently sold just the contact assembly to a customer who then inserted it into a housing.[15]

The royalty issue never became an obstacle, however, because ITT Cannon was at the time interested in manufacturing a version of AMPMODU, the printed circuit inter-connection system AMP had developed in the 1960s and which had become an industry standard. In mid-1972, a cross-licensing deal was struck whereby AMP was granted the right to produce AMPLIMITE connectors and ITT Cannon the right to produce AMPMODU.[16]

The way now clear for commercial marketing, AMPLIMITE connector sales took off immediately. Initially used in avionics, AMPLIMITE connectors saw their first real commercial boost come with a 25-position version developed in 1972 to meet the industry standard for a connector used in modems and other data transmission devices.[17]

But the real launching pad was provided by an unlikely source: a representative from a small video game company called Atari approached AMP in 1973 to discuss the possibility of adapting AMPLIMITE connectors for use in a home video game.

Privately, Rundle was skeptical.

"I thought it was a total waste of time," he said, assuming AMPLIMITE would be too expensive for a small project like this.[18]

But the games Atari came out with in the 1970s included the wildly popular Space Invaders. AMPLIMITE connectors did indeed wind up in Atari video games and spread quickly to many other applications, notably to computers.

Annual AMPLIMITE connector sales catapulted from about $200,000 in 1972 to more than $14 million in 1976.[19]

Interesting was a process developed to reduce waste by using metal more efficiently when stamping terminal parts from strip metal.

ITT Cannon's half of the bargain did not work out nearly so well, since it was not equipped to produce AMPMODU connectors in anything like the volume AMP could. In retrospect, the patent swap was a windfall for AMP.[20]

Aside from its eventual profitability, the deal was also significant in that it marked a departure from AMP's long-held policy against licensing agreements. In this case, the sharing of a proprietary product, which was heresy in the early days of the company, turned out to be a very wise decision.

The Telecom Division

Although G. Earle Walker had observed as early as 1948 that "millions and millions of terminals must be used by the telephone and telegraph companies," it wasn't until the 1970s that AMP became a heavyweight contender in the industry.[21]

Prior to the 1960s, AMP wasn't large enough to attract the attention of the communication giants, who needed assurance that a supplier could reliably deliver the huge quantities of connectors required.[22] Also, telecommunications was largely confined to transmission of voices over wires, and switching technology was electro-mechanical, which meant that industry giants like Bell and Western Electric could manufacture their own terminals.[23] In the mid-1960s, AMP established a foothold in the telephone and power and utility industries with the introduction of its PICABOND and AMPACT product lines, which were designed to speed up connections in the field for telephone servicemen and power lineman.

In the late 1960s, however, vast new markets for connectors opened when Bell and Western Electric began to convert their national switching network from electro-mechanical to solid state. Recognizing this opportunity, AMP established a new marketing division, Telecom, in 1972. Herman Haas was put in charge.[24]

Joseph Brenner, who inherited the position of CEO in 1972, was optimistic about AMP's future in telecommunications. "We expect to be a major sup-

plier to Western Electric, Automatic Electric and other telephone equipment manufacturers, particularly in their transition to electronic switching," he said in a May 1972 trade magazine interview.[25]

He was correct. The Telecom Division achieved a 25 percent yearly growth rate in the 1970s,[26] and in less than a decade, communications rose from just a few percentage points of AMP's overall business to more than 15 percent.[27]

Among the products adapted for the telephone industry in the 1970s was the CHAMP connector for 25-pair telephone cables, which could be applied economically in high volume with AMP tools and semi-automatic machinery. It was used extensively in telephone switching panels. AMP also began marketing connectors for telephones themselves as well as for answering machines and PBX equipment. Meanwhile, it continued its production of connectors and application tools for installation and maintenance of telephone cables in the field.

AMPLIMITE connectors got a needed boost when they found practical applications in the wildly popular mid-1970s video games.

Foreign Expansion

AMP's success during the 1970s was remarkable when compared to other domestic corporations, but made sense when the company's global reach was factored in. Throughout the decade, AMP opened new global markets on a regular basis and came to rely on the profits that foreign subsidiaries were pumping home. As early as 1970, AMP's foreign operations contributed almost half of the company's net income (nearly $12 million out of the $24.5 million total) and all of its growth, reflecting the fact that foreign markets for electrical components were growing faster than domestic.[28]

By 1973, AMP had "by far the best foreign profitability" (60.5 percent of the total profit picture came from overseas) of any major electrical/electronic equipment company,[29] and as company sales soared through the 1970s, foreign subsidiaries continued to contribute about half of total revenues. In the three-year period between 1976 and 1979, for example, AMP doubled its overseas sales.[30] By the

end of the decade, AMP operated subsidiaries in 22 countries, nine of which were added in the 1970s: Argentina and Brazil (1971); Switzerland (1973); Finland (1976); Norway and Singapore (1978); and Belgium, Hong Kong and New Zealand (1979).

In those days, there was a definite laissez faire attitude toward the overseas companies, with subsidiaries handling their own marketing and sales, and in some cases, manufacturing. Europe, for instance, was a freewheeling and open environment, according to Dennis Morse, who rose to the rank of managing director for AMP Great Britain. European companies were free to set up their own protocols and enjoyed a "free exchange of information between companies."[31]

The relationship between engineering, sales and marketing was structured vertically, remembered Gerry Schmidt, corporate vice president, AMP Europe. "We organized teams vertically. We had one for auto, one for consumer electronics,

Left: AMP products found their way into a variety of telecommunications products, including these decorator telephone models by American Telecommunications Corporation.

Below: CHAMP connectors, shown in Nippon Electric PBX equipment, could be installed quickly and inexpensively using AMP insulation displacement technology.

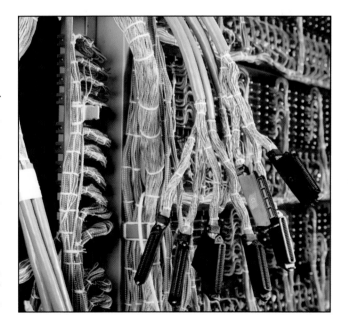

Above: AMP was active in the overseas automotive market and developed products for a variety of uses in foreign cars.

Right: In 1976, AMP began supplying foreign automakers with central junction units for electrical systems, such as for Fiat.

to a combination of "severe price competition," as well as "eccentricity" on the part of major French automakers Renault, Peugeot and Citroen.[33]

The situation was the same in the Far East, particularly in Japan, where the traffic situation was described as "frightful" in company minutes. "The only good thing about the deplorable traffic conditions is that 90 percent of the vehicles have AMP terminals in them."[34]

The key to success in Japan, according to Jean Gorjat, corporate vice president of the Asia Pacific region, was quality. "AMP in the Far East means product engineering. So one of the first things was to set up product engineering departments in the other countries as quickly as possible."[35]

AMP Japan was the launching point for the company's expansion into the rest of the Far East. And it was an exceptionally stable launching pad. AMP had founded its subsidiary in Japan in 1957 and has been credited with being one of the first American companies to penetrate

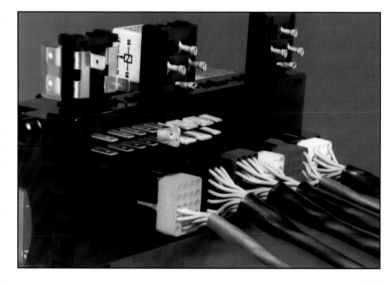

one for the appliance industry, and of course the electronics business as it was then known. We had three separately managed engineering departments that were closer to sales than their own chief engineer."[32] Later, these vertical organizations within companies, which came to be known as "silos," would be replaced with the matrix organization concept of highly functional teams that cut across boundaries.

AMP was particularly strong in automotive markets abroad. By the early 1970s, AMP dominated the automotive markets in Europe and Scandinavia, with an almost 100 percent market share in Sweden and Holland, 95 percent in Italy, 90 percent in Spain, and 65 percent in Great Britain and major customers in German auto producers, including Volkswagen, BMW, and Mercedes. Only in France (25 percent) was the company judged to have a "less than satisfactory" penetration in the early 1970s. This was attributed

the Japanese market.[36] In the earliest days, AMP was forced to overcome the Japanese resistance to outside companies by forming the Oriental Terminal Products company, which was officially AMP's licensed distributor in Japan. This set up the interesting situation where AMP was selling terminals to itself before it could turn around and sell them to customers. That changed in the early 1960s, when AMP Japan went to direct sales, which Bob Nishiyama, who was general manager of AMP Japan from 1968 until 1985, credits with AMP Japan's explosive growth.

Nishiyama's story itself is symbolic of Japan's incredible rise into the top tier of industrialized nations during the 1970s and following decades. In World War II, Nishiyama served as a fighter

Above: An AMP plant in Barcelona, Spain, began operation in 1971.

Right: In 1976, AMP opened a facility in Sao Paulo, Brazil, signalling AMP's movement into South America.

pilot for the Imperial Japanese Navy. Near the end of the war, he was called upon to sacrifice himself in a kamikaze mission, but the war fortunately ended before he was sent to his death.

Robert Stansbury Johnstone, an 18-year-old American soldier stationed in the Philippines, was not so fortunate. The young American died in fighting on Luzon. Just before he died, however, he wrote to his parents suggesting that they use the money from his government insurance to set up a scholarship fund so America's enemies could be schooled at American schools and see the American way of life.[37]

Bob Nishiyama was the first recipient of a Johnstone scholarship. He left Japan in 1947 and attended Lafayette College in Easton, Pennsylvania. After graduation, he went back to Japan and signed on with AMP in 1958.

Nishiyama's cross-Pacific qualifications were unique at the time, which helped him understand the special challenges that faced salesmen in

Japan. In America, AMP salesmen had to convince customers that crimping was better than soldering. The sale ultimately rested on that point coming across clearly. It was different in Japan.

"There was a comparison chart for if you terminated terminals through a classical way of soldering, the cost would be so much because soldering takes a lot of temperature control. If you used AMP, you'd save so much. But that chart didn't work in Japan because the Japanese people are much faster and much better at soldering."[38]

Instead, the Japanese unit made an aggressive foray into the terminal-intensive automotive market, where harnesses were coming into popular use. It worked and AMP jumped from that industry into consumer electronics, and into computers. This model would prove successful in many Asian markets throughout the 1970s and 1980s.

Penetrating New Markets

In 1971, Jean Gorjat was working in Spain and received the mission to set up shop in Brazil with Dominique Chavin. Gorjat was just the man for the job. Over the course of his 35-year career with AMP, Gorjat, reporting to International Division head Gerry Englehart, helped open up new markets in three continents, including South America, Europe and Asia.

Chavin joined AMP in 1964 as an assistant materials director before transferring to AMP de France and eventually rising to general manag-

U.A. Whitaker died in 1975 after 34 years at the head of AMP.

allowing him and his team to attend a trade show in Moscow.

"AMP participated in the Electro '72 exhibition in Moscow. It was really the first very important electrical exhibition in any of the eastern European countries since World War II, and I got AMP Germany interested in this. We hired a booth at the exhibition, and we exhibited there for something like two weeks during the month of July, which, if I remember well, was one of the warmest months in the history of the town. I'm pleased to say that we had a lot of success because we were presenting something which the people in the Soviet Union had never seen or even dreamed of, solderless wire connections."[40]

Of course, the group never got an order, but the move attracted a lot of attention throughout AMP, including a visit by Whitaker himself. Whitaker supported Tsygalnitzky, but would not allow a Russian manufacturer to be licensed to produce AMP products. Nevertheless, when AMP was later ready to move into former communist countries, the company's name was already known.

Boom and Bust

After modest sales growth of 6 to 7 percent per year in 1970 and 1971, AMP sales blossomed. The extraordinary growth began with the last quarter of 1971 and ended with the second quarter of 1974. Sales more than doubled over this span, from $239.6 million in 1971 to $482.1 million in 1974, with 1973 showing one of the largest annual increases in company history: 38 percent.[41]

Although business was good in all AMP markets, the heavy demand for connectors in computers and business equipment was largely responsible, accounting for 40 percent of the sales increase between 1972 and 1974.[42]

The electronics boom of the early 1970s, unfortunately, had a whiplash effect on component manufacturers like AMP. During the boom, OEMs stocked up on components such as semiconductors and connectors, building inventories

er of AMP de France and AMP Brazil. "In Brazil in those days, inflation was running somewhere between 30 and 40 percent a month and up to 100 percent a month. So our sales force was spending about half its time just negotiating price increases."[39]

Although it would not come to fruition for years, the groundwork also was laid for AMP's entry into eastern Europe in 1972. At the time, the Cold War was in full bloom, meaning that American trade with Eastern bloc countries was not encouraged. However, AMP intuitively recognized the future value of business behind the Iron Curtain. George Tsygalnitzky, AMP director of Export in London, talked AMP Germany into to meet the high demand. Then in 1975, America plunged into a recession during which the economy nearly ground to a halt.

A *Forbes* magazine analyst observed, "Inventories got even fatter after the Arab oil embargo of 1973. When the recession hit, customers quickly discovered they had enough electronic components to last them for quite some time. So instead of orders trailing off gradually, customers stopped buying abruptly."[43]

AMP began to feel the effects in the second quarter of 1974, and the downturn continued until the latter part of 1975, when sales began to pick up again. Overall, the company suffered a 15 percent drop in sales for 1975, only the third sales decline in its history (the other two being the postwar year of 1946 and the recession year of 1958). Layoffs were heavy as employment was reduced to 12,500 in the first quarter of 1975.[44]

On September 16, 1975, toward the end of this sales slump, U.A. Whitaker, who had a history of heart trouble, died of a heart attack at his vacation home on Swan's Island off the coast of Maine.[45] The Coronary Club, a group Whitaker founded for heart attack victims, published a large photo of him on the cover of its November 1975 newsletter, with the following tribute: "A rare person, simple, understanding, generous and extraordinarily competent, he represented the best in the successful businessman. Our American democracy would be safe in the hands of such a man."[46]

At the October meeting of the AMP board, Cleve Fredricksen was elected chairman to replace

Above: After Whitaker's death, long-time AMP employee Cleve Fredricksen was elected chairman of the board in October 1975.

Right: Willard Smith was an AMP board member and appeared to be heading for the presidency. Tragically, he died of cancer in 1979.

Whitaker. Also elected to the board were two 20-year men being groomed as future heads of the company: Walter Raab and Willard A. Smith.[47]

Tragically, Smith died at age 51 on April 24, 1979, after a short bout with cancer. A native of Centralia, Pennsylvania, Smith had risen steadily through the ranks after joining AMP in 1950.[48] In 1968 he was named vice president of European Operations, and in 1971, vice president in charge of Manufacturing and Product Planning. Smith was noted for his contributions to technical innovation and new product development and was highly respected by peers and employees.

Chet Timmins, who began working for AMP in 1959, was hired by Willard Smith after a summer college internship. In an interview, Timmins recounted Smith's contributions.

"I have much admiration and respect for Willard Smith, and it was unfortunate for this company that he had an early death. I thought Willard was not only a leader, but an innovator searching for new better and different ways. He had a quiet way with people. He was able to persuade them and convince them to do more and better. I feel as though I learned a lot from him."[49]

Domestic Expansion

As the company opened subsidiaries around the globe, it continued to expand its manufacturing and engineering facilities at home. To a large extent, domestic manufacturing supported the foreign sales expansion. "Approximately 20 to 25 percent of the sales of [foreign] subsidiaries is of products produced here in our U.S. plants and exported to them for further processing or for direct resale to their customers."[50]

AMP steadily added to the sprawling Harrisburg campus near its headquarters on Eisenhower Boulevard. In 1972, a 100,000-square-foot administrative building was opened on a 125-acre tract along Fulling Mill Road. Also during the seventies,

AMP Special Industries set up this self-service display at Cumberland Electronics in 1974 as part of its new push to reach small customers.

three large engineering buildings were erected on a 128-acre tract across the street from administration, less than two miles from headquarters, the last opening in 1980.[51]

In 1973, AMP expanded into Virginia with a 33,000-square-foot manufacturing plant in Weyers Cave. By 1979, AMP occupied 50 facilities in central Pennsylvania and more than 20 in North Carolina, South Carolina, Florida and Virginia.[52]

Evolution of Markets

One of the keys to AMP's success during the phenomenal growth of the 1970s was its continued ability to spread a relatively narrow product line into many fields. As CEO Joe Brenner said in 1974, "We have remained very specialized in product but broadly diversified in the industries we serve. That is the way we like to do business."[53]

This strategy would be adopted by all the major connector manufacturers that survived into the 1980s. As one industry analyst observed in 1979,

"The diversification into a number of markets rather than specialization has become a standard practice of the connector companies. Some such as Amphenol and Bendix are still heavily military

and aerospace oriented, but for the most part all connector companies have succeeded in freeing themselves of single-market orientation."[54]

In the mid-1960s, AMP first divided its markets into six broad categories, each of which then contributed between 10 and 20 percent of total revenue: aerospace and military; commercial and industrial electronics; computers and data processing; consumer goods; transportation and electrical equipment; and utilities, construction, maintenance and repair.[55]

Over the next 15 years, these categories often shifted and recombined. In 1973, for example, the markets were reduced to five when a new category, general electronics, was created to include military electronics and communications.

In 1976, maintenance and repair, which had evolved into maintenance, modernization, utilities and construction, was renamed special industries. In 1977, the categories expanded again to six when communications was identified as a separate market, reflecting AMP's expanded presence in telecommunications.

By the 1979 Annual Report, seven broad market categories were identified, along with their approximate worldwide sales: aerospace and military (5 percent); industrial and commercial electronics (10 percent); communications (15 percent); computer and office (20 percent); consumer goods (15 percent); transportation and electrical (20 percent); and special industries (15 percent).

An Industry Giant

By the end of the decade, AMP was the acknowledged leader in its industry, having eclipsed the $1 billion sales mark for the first time in 1979.

In only two decades, AMP had established itself as the premier multiple contact connector supplier worldwide. By 1979, the company controlled a 15 percent share of the $1.3 billion domestic connector market. Its nearest competitor, ITT Cannon, held 10 percent.[56]

Even as its sales grew toward the billion-dollar mark in the late 1970s, AMP was still investing upwards of 9 percent of sales in RD&E. A *Business Week* survey published in June 1977 listed AMP, at 9 percent, ninth among all American corporations in percent of sales spent on RD&E in 1976. Among electronics/electrical companies, AMP trailed only American Microsystems (9.6 percent). However, AMP's expenditure was the more impressive, given that American Microsystems sales were $67 million in 1976, compared to AMP's $522 million. The same survey showed AMP invested much more on RD&E than competitors Burndy (4.3 percent) and Molex (6.1 percent).[57] By the end of the decade, even though AMP sales had nearly doubled, the company was still spending 9.2 percent on RD&E.[58]

Remarkably, AMP had achieved its growth to this point without acquisitions. Rather, it continued to invest heavily in itself, expanding through wholly owned subsidiaries and plowing an industry-leading percentage of sales back into research and development.

Joe Brenner and Cleve Fredricksen look over plans for one of the new engineering buildings going up at the Fulling Mill Road site near Harrisburg in 1978.

The 1983 acquisition of Carroll Touch Systems brought AMP into the new field of touch screen data entry.

CHAPTER EIGHT

MORE THAN A BOX OF CONNECTORS

1980–1990

"It's no longer enough to just supply a box of connectors. ... The customers want you to supply completed cable assemblies, test them, and make sure that everything is perfect."

— Walter Raab, 1988[1]

AMP SPENT THE 1980s departing from some of its most cherished traditions. In the early years of Aircraft-Marine Products, U.A. Whitaker and his officers laid down some basic guiding philosophies: reinvest in the company, decentralize, use direct selling, stay away from government business, and above all, offer a quality product. Whitaker founded his company on the "Mom and apple pie" morality of the forties and fifties. In Ronald Reagan's eighties, that wasn't going to work. Business moved too quickly, technologies transformed almost overnight, and the competitive arena became so intense that corporate raiding evolved into a Wall Street spectator sport.

For AMP, continuing its prosperity meant that almost every one of Whitaker's guiding principles would be reexamined, then overturned. Every one, that is, with the notable exception of quality. The 1980s ushered in a new drive for quality. AMP was challenged to be the best in the industry, and then challenged to be better than itself.

Rather than an internal shortcoming, the new attitude reflected changes within the electronics industry — including shortened product life cycles and a reduction in the number of suppliers used by large OEMs — that forced AMP to adapt. The "Plan for Excellence," later to be renamed the "Journey to Excellence," was launched in recognition of these demands. Meanwhile, manufacturing processes and facilities were streamlined to accomplish the goals expressed by the 1980s catchwords "Just in Time" manufacturing and "Ship to Stock" status.

At the January 28, 1981, board meeting, the executive team that would lead AMP through the decade was put into place, beginning with the election of longtime CFO Walter Raab as vice chairman and the retirement of Cleve Fredricksen as chairman. Chief Executive Officer Joe Brenner replaced Fredricksen, assuming the dual roles of chairman and CEO. He would hold both titles for only a year, until he reached retirement age in 1982. On May 1, 1982, Walter Raab, then 57, was elected to both the open positions of chairman and CEO.

Unlike Whitaker and Brenner, Raab had no engineering or manufacturing background; like Fredricksen, he was a financier. His tenure marked a departure for AMP, which had the reputation of an engineering culture from top to bottom. But Raab fit the times. His tight cost accounting and creative restructuring helped the company weather a financially troubled decade.

The AMP Quality Pin became the symbol of the 1980s as the company pushed for better quality to meet technology's high standards.

President James Marley, left, pictured with vice chairman Harold McInnes in 1986.

"AMP's Chairman and CEO, Walter F. Raab, is characterized by an industry expert as being 'as dominant and as important within AMP as Mr. Knight is at Emerson and Mr. Welch is at G.E.' ... He held things together in tough times."[2]

Also in 1981, Harold McInnes was named president. A graduate in mechanical engineering from MIT, McInnes began with AMP in June 1965 in the Connector Product Division. He moved up the ranks in manufacturing, first in Packaging Components and then in Automachine. After heading General Products, he became divisional vice president, Manufacturing Resources, and then corporate vice president, Engineering and Technology Resources.[3]

Jerry Labowitz of Merrill Lynch, a leading analyst of the electronics industry, characterized the transfer of leadership as "a very smooth transition. It doesn't signal any major change in direction."[4]

Two executives who would eventually lead the company, James Marley and William Hudson, also moved up the ladder in the early 1980s. In June 1983, Marley became vice president of Operations, replacing John Eberle, who retired. In July 1983, Hudson was named to the newly created position of divisional vice president, Far East

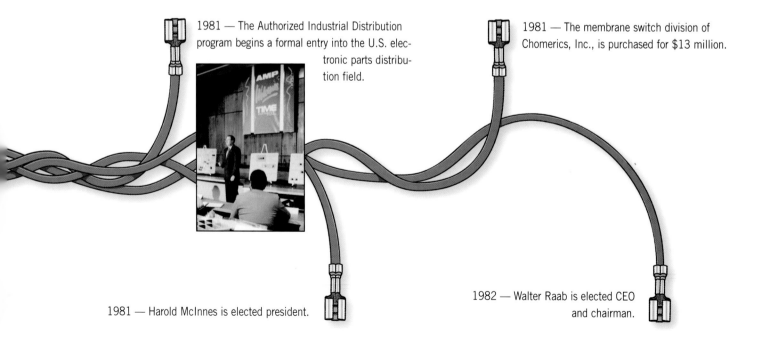

1981 — The Authorized Industrial Distribution program begins a formal entry into the U.S. electronic parts distribution field.

1981 — The membrane switch division of Chomerics, Inc., is purchased for $13 million.

1981 — Harold McInnes is elected president.

1982 — Walter Raab is elected CEO and chairman.

Operations, reporting to Gerry Englehart until 1988 when Englehart left the company.[5]

Overall, the decade was a rocky one for the electronics industry in general, and AMP did not escape the boom-bust cycle. The recession of 1981-82 kept earnings flat, while the sharp downturn of 1985 was the most severe market correction ever seen in the electronics industry. Despite the fact that AMP recorded a drop in earnings in 1982 and 1985, however, the company rebounded from both slumps and nearly tripled its sales, from $1 billion in 1979 to $2.8 billion in 1989.

More Than "A Box of Connectors"

The engine that drove AMP's quality movement in the 1980s was more than a desire to improve teamwork, empower workers and renew pride in craftsmanship — although it did accomplish these goals. The real impetus was a fiercely competitive business environment in which manufacturers were shrinking inventories, reducing their number of suppliers, and demanding higher quality parts and better service from those that remained.[6]

Furthermore, it suddenly became possible (and economical) for virtually anyone to ship a package from New York to Los Angeles overnight. The industrial equivalent, Just in Time manufacturing, meant that manufacturers wanted only as many parts as they could use immediately. The days of warehouses filled with inventory were ending.

Another 1980s trend was "Value Added" product. Citing the trend toward Value Added product in a 1988 *Financial World* interview, Walter Raab said, "It's no longer enough to just supply a box of connectors. ... The customers want you to supply completed cable assemblies, test them, and make sure that everything is perfect."[7] AMP's nickname for selling in this environment was "selling up the food chain."

Speed and quality became a matter of survival for component manufacturers like AMP, according to James Marley, vice president of Operations.[8] As manufacturers reduced their number of suppliers, those that couldn't deliver quality products quickly were the first to go. In fact, between 1982 and 1986, many large OEMs reduced suppliers from thousands to hundreds, according to Russ Knerr, then vice

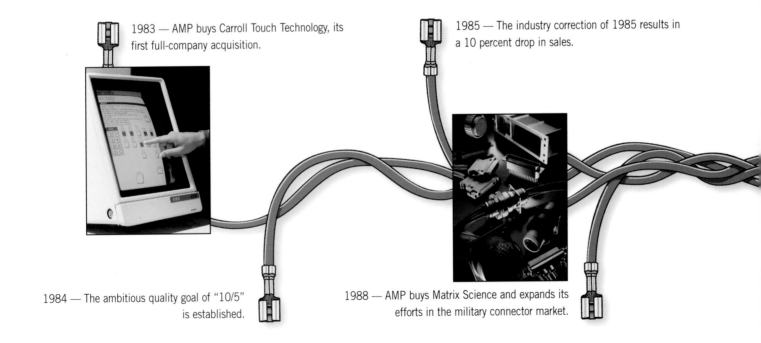

1983 — AMP buys Carroll Touch Technology, its first full-company acquisition.

1985 — The industry correction of 1985 results in a 10 percent drop in sales.

1984 — The ambitious quality goal of "10/5" is established.

1988 — AMP buys Matrix Science and expands its efforts in the military connector market.

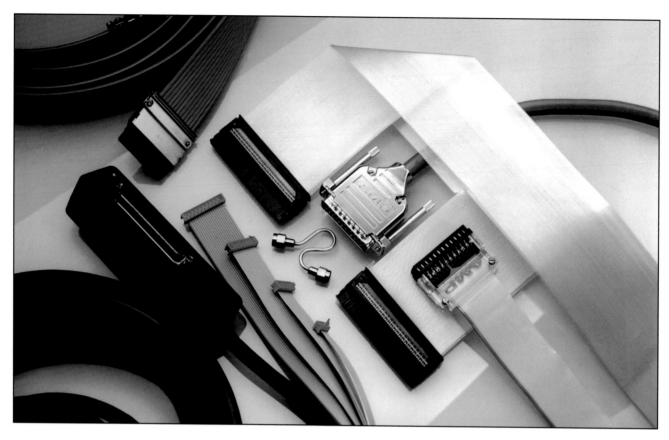

president for AMP's Information Systems marketing group.[9]

Consequently, AMP had to accelerate production, which meant streamlining and consolidating manufacturing processes; preassemble more components; and also improve the quality of its products to Ship to Stock status, so that a customer could install them without testing. Reduced inventories placed an added emphasis on quality: If a part was defective, there was no back-up component on the shelf.[10]

Value Added manufacturing, which was a different concept from value added product, meant eliminating any step in AMP manufacturing — such as inspections of a product at different stages in different plants — that added cost without adding value to the product. The pressure to deliver preassembled, defect-free products more quickly and efficiently forced AMP to modify its traditional commitment to small factories. Integrating processes and consolidating plants was one way to achieve this goal, and AMP was forced to comply, noted Harold McInnes.

AMP began offering more "Value Added" products, like the cable assemblies shown here, in the 1980s in response to a growing preference among large OEMs for complete assemblies, which saved labor costs and improved quality.

"We are consolidating into newer, more efficient facilities, but it's still the exception that we have a plant with more than 300 production people. ... We don't have too many plants with only 50 or 60 people but we've tried to keep 300 the upper limit."[11]

AMP first experimented with integrated manufacturing in its Gaffney, South Carolina, plant, and the experiment was so successful the entire operation was moved to American Avenue in Greensboro, North Carolina. Herb Cole was put in charge of starting the facility.

"We closed three or four different plants and moved everything under one roof. To start with,

they were almost in the red, but in just 18 months they were making a very nice profit. We credit most of it to consolidation, Just in Time or Value Added concepts, and having the people all under one roof where they can get quick answers, not have to rush back and forth, and can eliminate redundant inspections."[12]

AMP's attention to manufacturing paid off. By 1988, according to *Financial World*, AMP was a "qualified or preferred supplier for virtually all its customers, and [had] moved to become a leader in so-called Ship to Stock programs."[13]

The Quality Program

At least in one respect, AMP was ahead of the times. Well before "Total Quality Management" (TQM) and "Continuous Quality Improvement" (CQI) were absorbed into the lexicon of the corpo-rate world, AMP had established a quality pro-gram of its own.

The thrust began in January 1981, when AMP named Dave Myers to the newly created position of product assurance director and charged him with finding ways to improve quali-ty in both the design and manufacturing phas-es.[14] In 1983, AMP formally initiated a company-wide quality improvement program designed to improve processes to prevent problems in the first place, rather than catch the defects at the end of the line.

At the start of the program, 100 managers were sent to Philip Crosby's Quality College in Orlando, Florida, to learn quality management techniques. The quality program eventually involved all the employees in the company.[15]

The next step came in 1984 when AMP set the ambitious goal of its "10/5 program": to reduce errors and defects by tenfold over the next

AMP graduates of the June 1982 "Executive Class" of the Philip Crosby Quality College. Pictured are (front row, from left) Dick Taylor, Jerry Byrem, Herb Stouffer, Jim Wagner, Crosby trainer Larry McFadden, Dick Brunner, Jerry Wisdo, Dave Cornelius and Al Schuck; (back row, from left) Gary Zimmerman, Jim Steeley, Fred Wahl, Bill Peterson, John Hayes, Bill Narigan, Bob Jones, Larry Fegley, Ron Hartwell, Conway Williams, Earl Hennenhoefer, Joe Sweeney, Homer Henschen and Burt Hendricks.

five years. In 1988, having achieved that reduction, management upped the ante, seeking
another tenfold improvement by 1990.[16] After
studying AMP's program in the spring of 1989,
Fortune's Bill Saporito wrote: "This is not a campaign consisting of slogans and buttons but a
highly technical program measuring some 50
variables across all functions from engineering
through secretarial. So far AMP has lowered its
'cost of quality,' the amount spent getting things
right, from slightly more than 16 percent of sales
to about 10 percent."[17]

Another program designed to improve service
was "Scorecard," established in 1987 to track
delivery times. On-time deliveries, defined as up
to three days early and zero days late, increased
from 65 percent in 1987 to more than 90 percent
by 1989.[18]

AMP Begins to Buy

AMP was more than 40 years old before it
acquired its first company; it had been an article
of faith since 1941 that AMP remain self-con-
tained. The eighties changed that, but nothing
could affect the core philosophies and conserva-
tivism that had built AMP. It was a manufacturing and engineering company first and foremost
and only acquired companies that company officers believed would broaden AMP's product line
and expertise. The fact remained that the electronics industry was moving too quickly for any
one company to keep up with. It became cheaper
to buy a company with a specialty than to develop the technology in-house.

As *Electronic Buyers' News* observed in
1986, "The connector industry is undergoing a
period of change marked by consolidation
through acquisition. Acquisition seems to be
the best route for established connector makers
to broaden their product line offerings and thus
maintain or increase overall market share."[19]
Or, as Walter Raab colorfully put it near the end
of the decade, "We're hanging onto the tail, and

In 1987, AMP's troubled subsidiary, AMP Keyboard Technologies,
offered a wide range of membrane switch and keyboard assemblies.

the tail gets bigger and goes faster, and that to which it's attached also goes faster, and this is the general electronic computer information systems market."[20]

Technically, AMP's first major acquisition was financial, a stock deal with Midland Investment Company finalized in April 1981 in which Midland stockholders became direct holders of AMP stock and Midland ceased to exist. (Midland was the investment company that had originally provided venture capital to launch AMP in 1941. Its assets in 1981 consisted mainly of AMP stock, of which it held 5,230,000 shares.)[21]

AMP's first significant technological acquisition, however, was its purchase of the membrane switch and keyboard division of Chomerics, Inc., also in April 1981, for $13 million.

Chomerics, based in Woburn, Massachusetts, was a manufacturer of specialty materials for electronic packaging, including "shielding, insulating and conductive materials, laminates and heat shrinking materials." Of its total $31 million in sales in 1980, $12 million were from membranes, making it the industry leader in the field.[22]

AMP's specific goal in buying the Chomeric Division was to gain faster entry into what seemed a promising technology: full-travel membrane keyboards. "Full-travel" refers to keys that move downward when struck, like those on a standard typewriter, the type of key action preferred by professional typists. Basically, standard keys are mounted over a polyester membrane which has been treated with conductive silver ink. When a key is struck, a connection is made which transmits the stroke to a computer monitor.

Included in the deal was Chomerics's 117,000-square-foot plant in Brattleboro, Vermont, and about 250 employees.[23] AMP created a subsidiary, AMP Keyboard Technologies (AKT), to develop the new product line, with

Jack Usner as marketing director and Chuck Wyrick as general manager. "I think AMP saw in Chomerics a technology that would have taken AMP a long time to get. It was a springboard for us to move into a market that's big and growing," Usner said in an interview shortly after the acquisition.[24]

However, the move did not prove fruitful. Early on, AMP discovered that the full-travel, low-profile keyboard Chomerics claimed to have perfected needed extensive redesign. "We pretty much had to start all over with that keyboard," an AMP spokesman said. "[Chomerics] misrepresented the stage of development of the products we acquired from them."[25]

AMP sued Chomerics for $10 million for breach of contract but later dropped the suit when Chomerics was acquired by W.R. Grace & Company in 1985.[26]

In September 1985, AMP decided to quit the full-travel membrane keyboard business, citing an inability to compete with foreign manufacturers. The AKT membrane plant in Burlington, Massachusetts, was closed, and one-third of membrane employees were laid off.[27]

An AMP spokesman told *Electronic News* the membrane operation "had not been profitable," and that despite many attempts at redesign, there were technical problems with the membrane switch that would require a "heavy investment" to correct.[28]

In 1989, AMP washed its hands of the venture and sold the AKT subsidiary.[29]

Other Acquisitions

In July 1983, AMP acquired 60 percent of Carroll Touch Systems and eventually pur-

Early in the decade, AMP purchased the membrane and switch division of Chomerics, which brought "full-travel" membrane keyboards into AMP's product portfolio. The venture was not successful.

chased the outstanding percentage. It was AMP's first acquisition of an entire company. Unlike many acquisitions during the eighties, AMP left Carroll's management intact.

Founded in 1974 by Champaign, Illinois, entrepreneur Arthur B. Carroll, Carroll Touch pioneered development of infrared scanning technology that allows a user to enter data by touching a

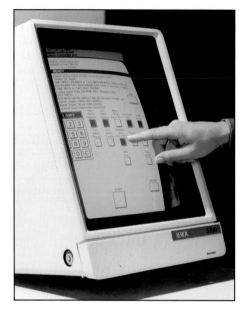

Above: The monitor of the 1983 Xerox 5700 laser printer was built with a touch screen made by Carroll Touch Systems.

Below: A Carroll Touch data entry screen, along with many other AMP products, was used on a blood analyzer made by Abbott Laboratories in 1988.

screen.[30] "The Carroll system essentially employs an infrared scanning system that sends beams of light across a screen in an X-Y grid pattern. Breaking a beam with a finger or a pencil sends instructions to the processor."[31]

Although Carroll Touch was small ($3.6 million sales in 1982), the touch system was gaining acceptance in applications where untrained users needed to enter data quickly, such as public information systems (like the kiosks at Disney's Epcot Center) and also in the military and in retail businesses and medical offices.[32]

More acquisitions followed. In 1985, AMP acquired Mark Eyelet, Inc., of Wolcott, Connecticut, a leading manufacturer of precision miniature components, such as printed circuit board sockets.[33]

Employees of Time Electronics, a connector distributor, are shown at an AMP training seminar in 1988. While still reliant on direct sales, AMP in the 1980s acknowledged the value of distributors in its overall plans.

In 1989, the company acquired Garry Screw Machine Corporation of New Brunswick, New Jersey, and Decolletage S.A., of St. Maurice, Switzerland, both manufacturers of metal parts for coaxial cable connectors, with combined sales of $24 million that year.[34]

Finally in 1989, AMP acquired Lytel, Inc., of Sommerville, New Jersey, maker of electro-optical devices. AMP had originally purchased a minority stockholder position in the company in 1985 with an eye on the promising fiber optics market.[35]

Distributors

Another AMP article of faith: keep sales in-house. In the 1940s, the company had used manufacturer's representatives only until it could afford its own sales force, but since then had remained staunchly committed to direct sales, using distributors only to reach small customers in remote locations.[36] Said Ben Conner, who retired in 1988 as vice president of marketing after 35 years selling AMP products: "The importance of direct selling cannot be overestimated. You know everybody in the customer's organization from the janitor to the president if you are a good AMP sales engineer, and you opened those sacred doors."[37]

In the mid-1970s, however, Oscar Rudolph of API (which subsequently became AMP Special Industries) had begun using distributors for after-market sales. General Sales Manager Joe Maher commented that AMP's Special Industries' distributor program "blossomed quite nicely," and by 1980, AMP management began to consider the same tactics for the parent company.[38] Both Rudolph and Maher went on to become marketing vice presidents.

By the latter half of 1980, trade magazines were buzzing with rumors of an AMP distribution network, and in January 1981, the company unveiled its Authorized Industrial Distribution (AID) program, with plans to "franchise 'a limited number of local distributors' to include some widely used selections from its connector offering."[39]

In spring 1983, the Distributor Marketing Division was created to oversee a growing network

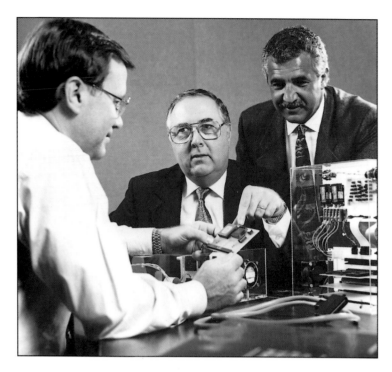

Above: AMP's Neal Spatz, center, vice president, distributor marketing, shows Hamilton/Avnet's Jim Smith, left, and Alex Mace, right, a training kit for the new distributor personnel.

Right: Pictured during a review of automated production assembly equipment in 1985, president Harold McInnes, left, and chairman/CEO Walter Raab.

By 1985, sales through distributors had reached 5 percent of total sales, and would double by 1988.[43] AMP's network of distributor locations grew to more than 1,000 in the latter half the decade. A significant milestone was reached in 1987 when every one of Hamilton/Avnet's locations was authorized and trained to sell AMP products.[44]

In 1988, AMP signed Kent Electronics in Texas, another outside distributor. By 1990, AMP was number one in U.S. connector sales through distributors.[45]

As with some of the other sea changes going on, reliance on distributors was brought on by the increasing demands of OEMs. Distributors offered a local source of products so a customer could quickly fill gaps in his inventory. They could also provide value-added services such as credit and assembly, as well as same-day delivery.[46] "The introduction of that program without incurring any major litigation was a challenge,"

of regional distributors.[40] Neal Spatz was named general manager of the new division and would eventually rise to vice president. According to Spatz, distributors offer certain benefits: a single source supplier, same-day delivery, and the ability to package products into one unit.[41]

Within the next year, AMP had signed with a select group of national distributors including Hamilton/Avnet Electronics, the largest electronic parts distributor, as well as with Marshall Industries and Schweber.[42]

But AMP was quick to put the new marketing strategy in perspective. In a press release announcing the Hamilton/Avnet agreement, the company said it would continue its "orderly expansion of distribution" but did not intend to change its marketing direction of addressing manufacturers with direct sales personnel.

AMP moved its global headquarters from Eisenhower Boulevard to new corporate headquarters at 470 Friendship Road in April, 1983.

remembered David Henschel, corporate secretary and associate legal counsel in 1997.[47]

The 1985 Correction

AMP had hit a billion in sales in 1979 and immediately headed into the recession of 1980-82, which kept sales flat at about $1.2 billion for two years running. Net income and earnings per share dropped 12 percent, only the fourth time in AMP history such declines had occurred, but it wasn't critical news.[48] Business rebounded in 1983 and 1984, posting sales increases of 22 and 20 percent, respectively, and showing even greater increases in earnings: 37 percent in 1983 and 23 percent in 1984.[49]

However, a $150 million jump in orders in the first quarter of 1984 set off alarms in the heads of AMP executives. They were witnessing the same pattern of overbuying and bloating that had occurred in 1974-75, just before the steepest one-year sales decline in AMP's history. In a statement accompanying the 1984 first quarter earnings report, Raab and McInnes characterized the surge as "highly unusual." They warned that it represented "far more than the normal seasonal strength and apparently included some customer overbuying and inventory buildup."[50]

The two executives displayed a highly perceptive grasp of what was about to happen. All around them, circumstances were rapidly aligning into a potent combination of factors that together would deal AMP its most serious blow so far.

First, an increase in the value of the U.S. dollar had the dual effect of discouraging export of American goods while boosting foreign competition in the U.S.[51] Many economists consider these years to be the arrival of global competition. As the dollar rose, U.S. manufacturers increased plant location overseas, becoming the first multinational corporations. Also, imported products became suddenly more affordable. Finally, AMP didn't have a price increase in 1984, one of the first times since the early 1970s. AMP had been the price leader in the industry, with a three or four percent increase every year. In 1984, however, foreign competition forced AMP to keep its prices stable.

Second, a bust in the electronics market occurred. The downturn coincided with the major transition in the electrical and electronics industry.

Customers were suddenly converting from "discrete components to larger subassemblies, from depending on cheap labor to advanced automation."[52]

The situation reached critical mass in 1985, resulting in the most severe correction the electronic industry had ever experienced. Wall Street analyst Stephen Roach termed it "the most protracted weakening of technology spending during the past 25 years."[53] AMP President Harold McInnes remembered the period.

"I can recall at the 1984 annual shareholder's meeting, explaining to shareholders, who were mostly financial analysts, all the things we were doing to accelerate the increase in manufacturing capacity. Then within about two months, we began to see the business just really hit the floorboards. Not only did bookings dry up, but orders were canceled and we had just a tremendous job of trying to react to that scenario. ... We had some very painful decisions to size ourselves appropriately to the levels of business that we saw for the foreseeable future."[54]

It couldn't have come at a worse time. The AKT full-travel membrane keyboard plant had just been closed, but AMP was still in a full-out buying mode, having just acquired Mark Eyelet, Inc. The company was also building to accommodate the extra business and in the middle of reorganizing its entire approach to quality management and manufacturing. AMP was in the midst of major spending projects and got caught in a capital spending mode that couldn't be helped, according to Walter Raab.

"We had to deliver the goods. We couldn't sit back and say no, even if we had thought the boom was going to go bust. We have learned that once you lose a good customer it takes years to regain his business, if ever. So we had to prime our production for the boom."[55]

Overall, in 1985 AMP sales fell 10 percent, with domestic sales recording an 18 percent drop. Worse yet, net income plummeted 46 percent while earnings per share fell 47 percent.[56]

The correction would hit AMP employees the hardest — layoffs and plant closings were the most drastic in its history. In one year, domestic employment was reduced by 2,700, about half through layoffs and the rest through attrition and voluntary severance plans. Several

Due to the Cold War buildup, the aerospace/military markets gained significance in the 1980s, initially with older connector lines, then with newer products, including ones made for Boeing. This collection of connectors all found application in the military/aerospace markets. The large connector in the left foreground is a Matrix Science military connector.

one-week furloughs without pay were imposed.[57] By 1987, the company was forced to close dozens of plants and reduce its U.S. workforce by 25 percent through attrition, early retirement and layoffs.[58] To reduce productions costs, the company opened a maquiladora manufacturing plant in Hermosilla, Mexico, which later became a wholly owned subsidiary.

All levels of the company were affected, recalled Merrill Yohe, who was assistant to the chairman at the time and rose to vice president of Public Affairs. "It addressed not only plant-related layoffs, but also white collar and to some degree middle management. ... It was the first time that we had developed human resource personnel policies to deal with all aspects of employment reduction, and it was important to the company's future that we do that."[59]

Phil Guarneschelli, then division vice president for Industrial Relations, said the period was one of his most challenging. "Even during those difficult periods, we used tools that basically emphasized voluntary behavior if we could. We tried to rely mostly on attrition and voluntary programs. Now, we did have some involuntary layoffs of significant magnitude, but they were only after we took every possible step we could on a voluntary basis."[60]

AMP recovered faster than the rest of the industry for a number of reasons. Already the leader in automated machinery, it had invested heavily in the development of pre-assembled, value-added components and so was better prepared than its competitors for the industry-wide conversion.

Furthermore, because of its size and reputation, AMP actually benefitted when OEMs began reducing suppliers to only the most qualified and reliable.

New Interest in Military Markets: The Matrix Acquisition

It was at the end of World War II that Whitaker had offhandedly remarked, "I certainly want to get into a business where I never would be required to sell the government anything."[61] The government wasn't the most cooperative of customers, and for the most part, AMP had stayed true to Whitaker's principle, doing modest business with the military during the Korean War,

then going after the consumer market with all its energy.

Then Ronald Reagan was elected and America embarked on the greatest peacetime military buildup in its history. The new U.S. weapons arsenal included such advanced technology as the F-18 fighter jet, the submarine-launched Trident nuclear missile, and the fearsome MX intercontinental ballistic missile. Merrill Lynch analysts predicted defense spending would increase 14 to 15 percent per year through 1985, "faster than in any period in the last 20 years."[62]

The analysts were correct. The worldwide market for military connectors rose sharply through the decade, reaching an estimated $2.5 billion by 1988. AMP found that it couldn't resist a market of this size.[63] In January 1987, it created a new business group, Federal Systems, headed by divisional Vice President Vincent Durkish.

In the summer of 1987, AMP began looking into acquiring the Matrix Science Corporation of Torrance, California, a leading maker of military connectors, with sales of $75 million in 1986.[64] AMP already was the leading supplier of commercial circular connectors, with a 27 percent share, but Matrix Science was the number four supplier of the military version, with an 8.8 percent share.[65] AMP officials met four times with Matrix between August and November, and by November 16, AMP had bought 988,300 shares (12.5 percent) of Matrix Science stock.[66]

AMP was not alone, however, in its interest in Matrix. Longtime competitor Molex had itself acquired 5.9 percent of Matrix Science stock by November 16. Late in the game, 3M entered the picture.[67] Everyone, however, had to wait for the outcome of an SEC investigation into Matrix's finances. Three top officials were eventually charged by the SEC for inflating sales reports in 1986-87 and were suspended by Matrix in August 1987, when the improprieties were discovered.[68]

As the investigation concluded, the companies engaged in a bidding war that AMP won. On May 23, 1988, Matrix and AMP arranged a stock swap, and AMP purchased Matrix for $113 million, according to the 1988 Annual Report.[69] The deal was finalized on August 17, 1988. The Fleck Report on the Connector Industry announced the acquisition.

"In the U.S., the acquisition of Matrix has a greater impact than it does worldwide. The deal combines Number One AMP, with a 15.8 percent market share, with Matrix, which ranks 14th among U.S. suppliers, with a 1.3 percent market share. The combination of the two firms will enable AMP to post over $1.1 billion connector shipments in 1988 (of the $2.67 billion of total sales). Thus 1988 will be a landmark year for the U.S. connector industry."[70]

A new organizational unit, the Aerospace/ Government Systems Sector, headed by vice president August Kastel, was created in 1988 to coordinate the operations of Matrix, the Federal Systems group and Carroll Touch.[71]

Increasing Emphasis on Global Markets

"Well, those were very interesting days," recalled McInnes. "In our domestic businesses then, we were still relatively free from interna-tional competition."[72] AMP was warned to watch for foreign competitors, however.

"One time we had the then-vice chairman of the board of Motorola come and talk with us. I think we were over a billion in sales then, and Motorola was closer to $10 billion, and he really gave us the early warning signal that we would soon see international competition here in the U.S. market. Some of the real challenges I think we went through in the eighties were when we began to cope with global competition."[73]

McInnes was right — but that didn't stop AMP from dominating the foreign markets it entered. In fact, AMP's global business snow-balled in the 1980s, actually eclipsing domestic sales in 1987 for the first time since the mid-1970s. By 1989, foreign subsidiaries contributed 54 percent of total sales.[74]

While production was scaled back at home, AMP was busy with plant openings and facility expansions overseas. New subsidiaries were opened in Austria, Denmark and Ireland (1980), Malaysia (1984), South Korea (1985), Taiwan (1987), Portugal (1988) and Switzerland (1989). Old problems, such as AMP de France's penetra-tion into the auto-maker market, began to turn

AMP purchased the Swiss screw machine company Decolletage S.A. St. Maurice, along with Gary Screw Machine Company in 1989. Pictured is screw machine production equipment in Switzerland.

around. And dozens of facilities were added or expanded upon in countries where AMP already operated.[75]

In Europe, Gerry Schmidt was vice president of central and northern Europe. Appointed in 1978, Schmidt expanded AMP's presence across those countries throughout the 1980s. In all, he established six companies: AMP Austria, AMP Switzerland, AMP Norway, AMP Denmark, AMP Finland and finally AMP Hungary. Schmidt organized his division vertically.[76]

Alfred Greger, who retired in 1994 as general manager of AMP Switzerland after almost 40 years with the company, worked with Schmidt in Europe in a variety of capacities. He remembered the 1980s, when he was working in marketing.

"We frequently had European marketing meetings in these beautiful cities of Europe. And I think these meetings were very successful. Schmidt organized the area meetings. ... He also founded the engineering groups. Those people not only engineered new connectors and terminals, but they also went to customers, they went out to meetings, they introduced new products, technologies, and so on. I think this was a very successful way of doing business."[77]

In addition to European operations, AMP began to expand across the Far East. In the early 1980s, things were going well in Japan, but not in the rising countries of Asia. AMP engineers were opening electronic products and discovering competitor's products. According to Bill Hudson, who became vice president of Far East operations in 1983, the domestic arm of AMP was worried about losing market share in the emerging industrial nations, but the International division insisted that AMP was doing well. "I was in the middle of that box," Hudson recalls.[78]

When Hudson arrived, momentum was not on AMP's side. There were competitor's plants already operating in Singapore and Taiwan. AMP itself had staff in Singapore, but was doing all its manufacturing in Japan and the vast majority of its revenue came from AMP Japan. Over the next eight years, Hudson opened nine

Ted Dalrymple, right, replaced W. Bennett Conner, left, as director of marketing when Conner retired in April 1988, shown within AMP's ShowMotion display van.

new manufacturing plants, including ones in Singapore, Korea and Taiwan. China and India would follow in the 1990s. Based on his performance in the Far East, Hudson was promoted to vice president of International in 1991.

At home, AMP's international division began to inherit more power. In November 1986, Gerald Englehart, formerly vice president of International, was elevated to executive vice president. James Marley, previously vice president of Manufacturing and Engineering, was elected AMP president, replacing Harold McInnes, who moved up to vice chairman of the board, with "broadened responsibilities in corporate administration and planning, and the long-term global aspects of our business."[79]

These changes were largely driven by the fact that AMP's biggest customers, the large manufacturers, were themselves becoming increasingly global and were demanding "identical products and services be delivered quickly to multiple locations."[80] Foreign subsidiaries were run very efficiently. In 1988, Merrill Lynch analyst Jerry Labowitz reported that "since 1975, AMP's international volume has grown five or six times, but employment overseas has grown only 30 percent."[81]

AMP continued its policy of staffing foreign subsidiaries with locals. "You need people who speak the language, know the customs and can recruit qualified people," Englehart said.[82]

Whatever AMP was doing abroad, it was working. By the end of the decade, AMP was "the largest manufacturer of connectors in every one of the 26 countries in which it operated, including Japan."[83]

AMP's Culture of Caring

Early on, AMP's new leadership made human resources a priority. In January 1982, a savings and thrift plan for U.S. employees was established, and the next year it was converted to a 401(k) plan. By 1985, 10,600 employees had signed up. The AMP 401(k) plan also enabled employees to purchase company stock.[84] The 401(k) plan evolved into a continuing success at AMP: By 1997, almost 16,000

Above: The 1980s ushered in a new era of technical training for more than 2,600 technical employees. This 1989 session is on electrical connector/contact design.

Right: Opto-electronic products in 1989 included, from left to right, an online data link module, an FDDI compatible transceiver, a single mode laser, and a miniature dual bypass switch.

employees, or 80 percent of the eligible employees, were participating in AMP 401(k) plans.

Former director of Investor Relations Bill Oakland, long a proponent of these moves, characterized them as "very important to the future of our employees."[85] Oakland started in investor relations for AMP in the late 1950s and spent nearly four decades at the head of the function for the company.

AMP also dramatically intensified employee training programs in the early 1980s. The training staff was doubled in 1984 alone, and regional training centers were established. By 1985, more than one-third of AMP employees were involved in some form of in-house or external skills or education program.[86]

Some of the education programs involved caring for the environment. Environmental consciousness emerged in the sixties. To do its part, AMP began working on environmental initiatives on an international basis. Carol Ritter, vice president of General Services, Engineering and Manufacturing Assurance, Americas, remarked that AMP "took it from primarily a U.S. focus to a global focus, and we've been recognized by a number of the agencies in the U.S. for having a very proactive environmental program."[87]

Finally, management in the early 1980s showed a general concern for communication with employees. The position of director of Employee Relations was created. Employee newsletters were published, as well as a quarterly magazine called *Connections*, which was written and edited by Dianna Reed, who went on to become manager of Community Relations and Contributions. Quarterly videos for employees were later added.

John Kegel, who started with AMP in 1978 and later became vice president, Logistics, Supplier Relations, ASG, and Strategic Tooling, said about AMP's general atmosphere:

"I have always known the chairman of the board on a first name basis, even when I was here only a year. Some people might say, 'Well, that's no big deal.' But I think it is a big deal because the relationship between the top guy on down is more intimate than the experiences that I've had working for a couple of other companies."[88]

Phil Guarneschelli, corporate vice president and chief Human Resource officer, credits the founder of the company with AMP's culture of caring:

"This goes all the way back to Mr. Whitaker. He respected people, and he respected the dignity of people whether they were in lower echelon jobs or higher echelon jobs. He treated people all the same, and I think that is basically the basis for why we have remained non-union for as long as we have here in the United States. Our people have never felt the need to have a third party between management and themselves."[89]

To keep abreast of the networking trend in the 1990s, AMP developed the AMPTRAC 16 Concentrator for Token Ring and Ethernet systems.

CHAPTER NINE

GATHERING EXCELLENCE

1990–1993

"Reliability must become the top issue in the 1990s."

—Harold McInnes, 1990[1]

B Y 1990, AMP was universally referred to as "the connector giant" in the press, a label that reflected its global dominance of the industry. With sales topping $3 billion in 1990 — more than half coming from overseas — AMP held about 18 to 20 percent of the worldwide market for electrical/electronic connection devices. AMP also led in market share over its old competitor, Molex, in the three major worldwide regions of the Americas, Asia/Pacific, and Europe.[2]

The company was in the enviable position of being number one in its field, able to afford a continuing, professional focus on RD&E, and able to fund what was important for the future.

Early in the decade, the company committed itself to the ambitious goal of growing at better than one-and-a-half times the predicted industry annual rate of 6 to 9 percent.

To achieve this growth, AMP would broaden and intensify the strategies established in the 1980s, which included acquisitions and joint ventures to gain access to new technologies and market opportunities; a "systems approach" to product development, emphasizing technologically advanced, value-added assemblies and interconnection systems, in addition to its traditional individual components; an increasing emphasis on global business and the increasing horizontal integration of global operations; and the expansion of the quality movement to include greater employee involvement and training, along with measurable standards in manufacturing at every site.

Harold McInnes and the Journey to Excellence

Harold McInnes, elected chairman of the board and CEO in 1990, was keenly aware of the sea changes in the connector industry and knew AMP would have to adapt. Addressing the International Connector Symposium in Toronto in October 1990, he said, "It is going to be a highly competitive environment where only the strongest will prosper and many will not survive."[3]

McInnes recognized that increasingly complex products demanded by customers would require connector companies to form technological alliances, to train employees more extensively than ever before, and to raise manufacturing to "equal status with R&D, marketing and finance after decades of second-class status."[4]

McInnes was particularly well suited to tackle these goals. Enthusiastic and congenial by nature, he had always emphasized quality

Harold McInnes was named chairman and CEO in 1990.

through teamwork. When McInnes took over as chairman of the board and CEO, he soon expanded the quality program he initiated as president in 1983 into a more sweeping program, formally named Journey to Excellence.

Launched in November 1989, Journey to Excellence adopted criteria used to judge winners of the Malcolm Baldridge National Quality Award. The plan placed heavy emphasis on employee involvement and training and also on measurable results in manufacturing and service. "It's proven itself for a decade now, and the best companies in the world follow Baldridge or similar quality criteria," noted Dean Hooper, vice president of Global Customer Satisfaction and Business Effectiveness, in 1997.[5]

Shown celebrating are winners of AMP's internal Journey to Excellence competition, AMP then-vice president of product quality Keith Drysdale, left front, congratulating unit winner Gary Gilbert of purchasing, ICCP Division in Greensboro, North Carolina. Standing are John Vandergrift (left), a team leader in ICCP, and Mike Hendy of the Communications Product Division.

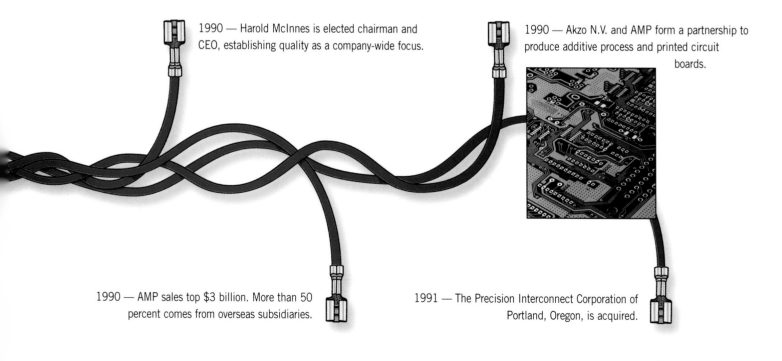

1990 — Harold McInnes is elected chairman and CEO, establishing quality as a company-wide focus.

1990 — Akzo N.V. and AMP form a partnership to produce additive process and printed circuit boards.

1990 — AMP sales top $3 billion. More than 50 percent comes from overseas subsidiaries.

1991 — The Precision Interconnect Corporation of Portland, Oregon, is acquired.

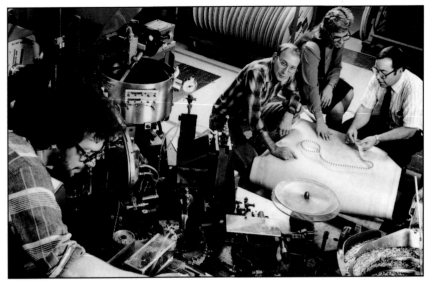

A product focus team representing several disciplines at the Jacobus, Pennsylvania, plant discusses application tooling in a 1990 meeting. AMP organized more than 500 teams as part of its Plan for Excellence.

Bill Narigan, who rose to vice president in charge of Corporate Quality, was instrumental in developing the program. He remembered pulling in leaders from all departments to engage in a six-month discussion on what excellence meant.

"In many ways, we had a little bit of excellence here and little bit over here and a little bit over there, and some people tooling around with it over here, and so forth, but nobody had ever put it together into a package and said how important this is to our company."[6]

One of the first moves was to cultivate a more collaborative work environment by increasing the number of project-focused employee teams. More than 500 were established worldwide by 1992. To heighten interest in employee quality efforts, an annual Excellence in Quality Improvement competition was established, in which 43 company organizations entered in 1993.[7] Training was another important element in the quality improvement movement. "A cornerstone [of the Journey to Excellence] is a quantum leap ahead in training, and our training expenditures have doubled in the last few years and will keep rising," McInnes said.[8]

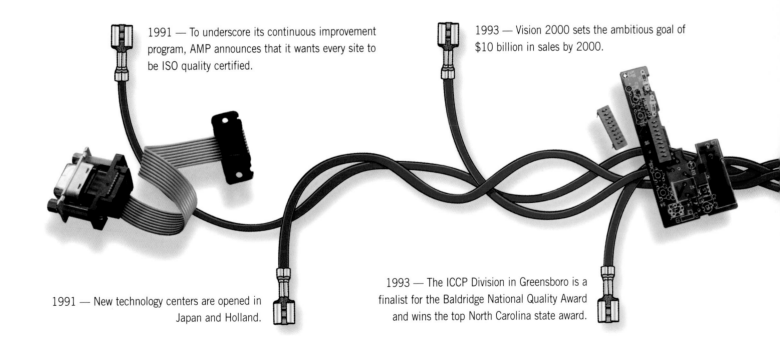

1991 — To underscore its continuous improvement program, AMP announces that it wants every site to be ISO quality certified.

1993 — Vision 2000 sets the ambitious goal of $10 billion in sales by 2000.

1991 — New technology centers are opened in Japan and Holland.

1993 — The ICCP Division in Greensboro is a finalist for the Baldridge National Quality Award and wins the top North Carolina state award.

Above: AMP maintains class 100, 1,000, and 10,000 clean rooms to develop cutting-edge technology.

Below: Through acquisition, product development and research contributions, AMP became a leading supplier of specialized cable assemblies.

The company goal was to provide each employee with a minimum of 40 hours of training in continuous improvement per year by the mid-1990s. Manufacturing employees would be judged against a seven-step Manufacturing Skills Inventory System to evaluate the level of training in each plant.[9] AMP further encouraged individual development by reimbursing employees for tuition for work-related courses from accredited colleges and universities.[10]

AMP also instituted the "Leaders of the Future" program, designed to identify and advance promising talent. Vice president of Global Succession and Organizational Planning Leonard Hill, whose background was in psychology and the theater, ran the program. "We're attempting to reach down into the very bowels of the organization. That is where your indicators of high potential are. ... These are people in their late 20s, early 30s, and in some way they have distinguished themselves."[11]

Plant Quality

AMP executives knew that improving individuals was not enough. The results of the various programs —

good or bad — had to be measured against both internal and external measuring sticks. So in 1991 AMP announced the ambitious goal of achieving ISO certification for every AMP manufacturing site.

Introduced in 1987 by the International Organization of Standards, ISO 9000 was a measure of a plant's quality control systems intended to give a customer assurance of a manufacturer's reliability. ISO certification was not then required by the market place, and only a handful of connector companies spent the time and money necessary to earn it.[12] By 1995, all of the company's significant manufacturing sites around the world had been certified.[13]

Henry Line, vice president of Global Standards, said ISO 9000 was costly but necessary. "ISO 9000 had been implemented in more than 17 countries. Some people say that ISO 9000 has become a $30 billion a year business, but also a large number of people in our business say that it's a very questionable return."[14] An even tougher rating to achieve was the MRP II, Class A rating. The Manufacturing Requirments Planning standard certifies excellence in materials requirements planning systems. By 1995, one-third of AMP plants had achieved this rating.[15]

AMP continued the drive for higher quality with the "Six Sigma" statistical goal — a maximum rate of three defects per million parts. But

Above: Long reliant on direct sales, AMP found that distributors and floor and counter displays could help sell its products.

Below: In the area of auto safety, AMP products were developed for air bags and anti-skid braking systems.

considering the industry standard was 3,000 defects per million, Six Sigma seemed to some analysts an unrealistic and unnecessarily expensive goal.

"That's hogwash," McInnes replied to such opinions.

"In everything we've done to date, our efforts to improve quality have yielded improved quality, higher productivity and lower cost. So the assumption that at the end of the day quality costs money is simply wrong. I suppose some people are only looking at the fact that you're going to have to invest to achieve this goal."[16]

The attention to quality paid off. In 1993, shortly after Bill Hudson was elect-

Above: Precision Interconnect of Portland, Oregon, makers of specialized cable and assemblies, was bought in 1991.

Below: This AMP slide switch was introduced as the smallest three-position switch on the market. It found a ready market in PC cards and garage door openers.

ed CEO, the Integrated Circuit Connector Products Division in Greensboro, North Carolina, was one of only four finalists among 32 entries to earn a site visit for the prestigious Malcolm Baldridge National Quality Award in the manufacturing category. A Kodak subsidiary eventually won the award, but the ICCP division won North Carolina's top quality award.[17]

AMP won many other quality awards from customers and industry groups in the 1990s. Its Williamstown/Tower City, Pennsylvania plants finished in the top 15 in *Industry Week's* 1993 "10 Best U.S. Manufacturing Plants" competition. The Automotive/ Consumer Business Group was voted best supplier among 500 others by the appliance industry for five years in a row. Dozens of companies, including AT&T, Ford, GE and IBM, rated AMP as the "best" or an "outstanding" supplier.[18]

Jim Marley, who would become chairman in 1993, saw the drive for quality as a way to bring AMP closer to its customers, and remembered how the North Carolina plant succeeded.

"I think the ability to focus on customers and to do the kind of customer work that generates new products is important. ... When we rolled out the Journey and created the Plan for Excellence, various entities throughout the company were embracing it in various ways. But when I found out that the fellas in North Carolina had made some really significant progress, I went down and spent a day with the team. I asked them how this all came about and largely they had done what I believed was fundamental for AMP going forward. They had created teams of people under one roof that had responsibility for all aspects of the business and they were able to drive through Value Added Manufacturing and through Journey to Excellence and quality programs to a level of performance in a business unit that AMP had never seen before."[19]

Right: ACSYS Products, AMP's networking division, offered concentrators, routers and intelligent hubs.

Below: Even as it moved into networking, AMP remembered its origins. Here, a LightCrimp tool is shown terminating a fiberoptic cable.

In December 1994, after 34 years with AMP, CFO Benjamin Savidge retired. Savidge had been named executive vice president in 1988 and elected to the board in 1989. He was replaced as CFO by Robert Ripp, who came to AMP in August 1994 after a 30-year career with IBM, where his last title was corporate vice president and treasurer.

AMP Keeps Buying

It was a big step when AMP moved into acquisitions during the eighties. But by the 1990s the

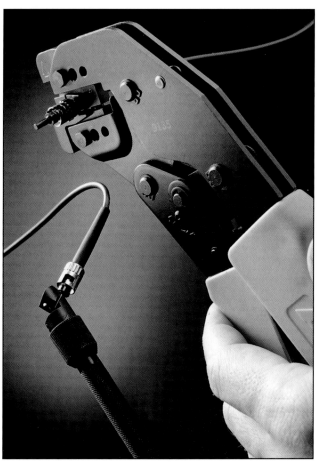

company pursued this strategy aggressively, acquiring companies and entering joint ventures at an incredibly rapid pace.

"Electronics companies are increasingly joining forces with other firms through consortia, joint ventures and other partnerships to shoulder the mounting risks and prohibitive costs of increasingly complex technologies," wrote one analyst in a 1990 industry survey.[20]

One force driving this trend was AMP's desire to offer customers "one-stop shopping" for all their connector needs, which meant broadening product lines and providing complete assemblies rather than discrete components.[21] A longer-term motive was the need to acquire new technologies, particularly in promising new fields such as additive printed wiring boards, fiber optics, interconnections and cable assemblies. Between 1990 and 1993, AMP used a variety of strategies, from

AMP France training manager Hervé Smith training Anixter employees on AMP products for the networking/customer premise market. Anixter is an AMP International distributor in the U.S. and Europe.

joint ventures to the purchases of product lines, divisions or even firms, to accomplish these goals:

- In 1990, AMP formed a joint venture with the Dutch chemical giant Akzo N.V. to produce additive process printed wiring boards (PWBs) for the computer, automotive and electronics industries.
- In May 1990, AMP bought a small fiberoptic firm, Kaptron, Inc., of Palo Alto, California, makers of passive fiberoptic components, test instrumentation and manufacturing equipment.
- In 1991, AMP acquired Precision Interconnect Corporation of Portland, Oregon, maker of specialty cable assemblies for medical electronics, test and mea-

surement equipment, high-end computing and high-speed digital transmission.

- In December 1991, AMP spent more than $5 million to purchase a 17 percent stake in BroadBand Technologies of Research Park Triangle, North Carolina, innovators in fiberoptics technology that enables cable and telephone companies to provide such services as video-on-demand and interactive shopping and banking.[22]
- In June 1992, AMP acquired Optical Fiber Technologies of Westford, Massachusetts, a manufacturer of precision metal ferrule fiber-optic connectors.[23]

Also in 1992, the company acquired Electro Optic Products, a DuPont division based in Research Triangle Park, North Carolina, and Netronix of Petaluma, California. These two companies were combined with AMP's Harrisburg-based networking business unit to form a new subsidiary, ACSYS, for marketing of value-added assemblies for the computer networking market.[24]

In its buying spree, AMP learned lessons from the past. Jim Marley added that with earlier acquisitions AMP imposed cost controls "from the large mother that the small child couldn't really afford."[25] In its next acquisitions, AMP took an almost totally hands-off approach that Marley didn't feel maximized AMP's results. "We are trying to focus more on what are strengths and weaknesses of the acquired company, where can we help it without imposing ridiculous extremes."[26]

The Sun Never Sets on AMP

AMP complemented its aggressive domestic acquisitions with its most ambitious program of overseas expansion to date, with most of the growth concentrated in the Asia/Pacific region and Eastern Europe.

Over the next few years, AMP added a dozen countries to its world map.[27] David Crockett, an industry marketing director for Europe, is credited with starting AMP's international marketing push. He believed that AMP's strong promotional value was the "very basic old AMP premise of the applied cost story." In other words, make sure people in whatever country understand that AMP's products cost less in the long run and they will convert.[28]

It worked. By 1990, foreign sales accounted for 59 percent of AMP's total. Thirty-five percent came from Europe, where AMP had nine manufacturing plants, and 19 percent from Asia/Pacific, where it had large plants in Japan, Taiwan, Korea and Singapore. It also had a small plant in Australia and sales offices in Hong Kong and Malaysia.[29]

In 1991, AMP committed itself further to its international operations and opened new technology centers in Japan and the Netherlands, driven by the leadership of Joe Sweeney, Javad Hassan, Gerry Englehart and Gerry Schmidt.

In 1992, the Whitaker Corporation was incorporated in Delaware with the mission of protecting AMP's intellectual property. "Our main goal is to protect AMP's huge RD&E investment around the world," said Jay Seitchik, president of the Whitaker Corp.[30]

Historically, the engineering brain trust had been centralized in Harrisburg, where innovations originated and were spread to the subsidiaries. Said future CEO and president Bill Hudson: "It created an environment where everybody was sitting back, waiting for these nuggets to come across the ocean so they could get going on to the next thing. The idea of focusing R&D in one country and ignoring the fact that technology was further advanced somewhere else was really setting us back in a strategic realm."[31]

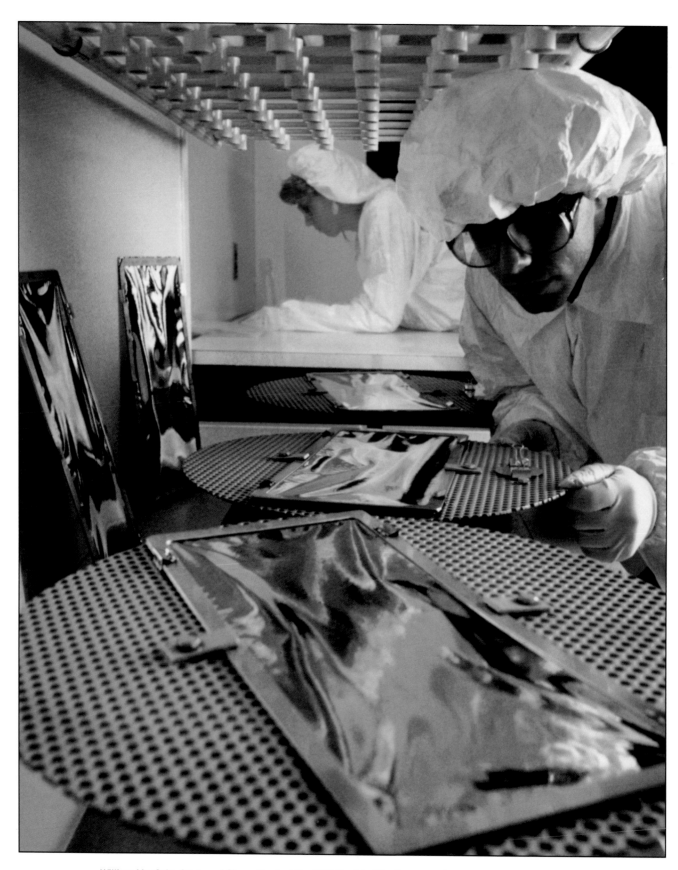

William MacCain, front, and Sherry Tuerk at the AMP Flexible Film Sensors unit in Valley Forge, Pennsylvania.

CHAPTER TEN

A GLOBAL VISION

1993–1997

"I think the position of the company now is to take advantage of the global nature of our business so that we are a more formidable global supplier."

—Jim Marley, 1988[1]

IN THE MIDDLE PART of the decade, AMP would undergo another change in leadership as it moved into yet another kind of business world. While the eighties were characterized by manufacturing and industry struggling to fit sleek new molds, the nineties can be characterized by the globalization of business and foreign competition. Acquiring the right technology became a paramount strategy as AMP continued to broaden its product line into advanced communications, greatly expanding its potential market.

Robert Ripp, who was hired in 1994 as chief financial officer after working at IBM, remembered his first impression of AMP as a company that "was in the midst of significant change."

"Since I've been here, it is clear that around the mid-1980s the industry became fiercely competitive. The old model of raising prices as a strategy to improve profit margins is no longer acceptable. With large customers demanding more from their suppliers and global competition investing so heavily to win market share, AMP had no choice but to formulate a new strategy. As I observe the strengths of this company, it is obvious that our core strength — AMP associates — will have to rise to the challenge to transform our culture to position AMP

to be the best connector company in our industry."[2]

Recognizing that the world was a smaller place — at least in terms of business — AMP integrated its global operations into industry-specific business units, which was part of Bill Hudson's plan. The regional mentality was gone. Switching to a "matrix" organization will pay off in the long run even if it requires extra effort to implement it, said Bill Oakland, former director of Investor Relations.

"You have geographic organization continuing and then you're adding product-oriented organizations such as cable, cable assemblies, optics, PC boards, and panel assemblies. Those are worldwide organizations that are product-based, technology-based. Then you're adding market-based units. And there is a marketing unit that also is worldwide — all added on top of the geographic organization. There are many people that have dual roles at least at this time where they continue in a geographic assignment and then take on one of these worldwide functions."[3]

AMP STACK connectors and hand tool, pictured in a Russian catalog.

Accordingly, new top leaders were chosen for their expertise to confront these challenges. Like Walter Raab, the financier who led the company through tough economic times in the 1980s, the top two executives of the 1990s would be chosen to lead AMP's global reorganization.

CEO Harold McInnes reached the mandatory retirement age of 65 in 1993, leaving the board with a difficult choice between two qualified leaders, William Hudson and James Marley.

Hudson, a native of Kenilworth, Illinois, and an electrical engineering graduate of Cornell University, started with AMP in 1961 and, beginning in the 1980s, lived in Tokyo and headed the company's Far East Operations for nearly a decade, where he was responsible for AMP's entry into new markets and explosive growth in Singapore. In 1991 he was named executive vice president of International Operations and elected to the board.

Marley, also a 30-year man, had an equally impressive track record in domestic operations. A

William Hudson became CEO/president in 1993, setting the company on a course of globalization.

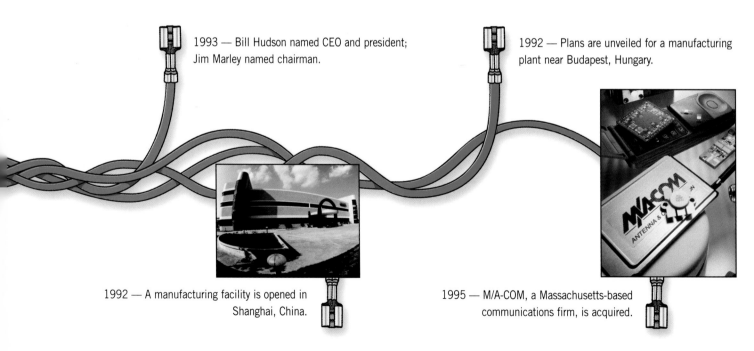

1993 — Bill Hudson named CEO and president; Jim Marley named chairman.

1992 — Plans are unveiled for a manufacturing plant near Budapest, Hungary.

1992 — A manufacturing facility is opened in Shanghai, China.

1995 — M/A-COM, a Massachusetts-based communications firm, is acquired.

native of Marietta, Pennsylvania, he held a bachelor's degree in aeronautical engineering from Penn State and a master's in mechanical engineering from Drexel University. He had succeeded John Eberle as corporate vice president of Operations in 1983 and in 1986 was named president and elected to the board.

Bernard Levine of *Electronic News* summarized the board's dilemma: "One helped build the firm's stellar international operations, the other successfully led the domestic business through a difficult restructuring in recent years. What to do?"[4]

The board's answer was to split the top jobs: Hudson was named CEO and president, and Marley, chairman of the board. Analyst William Milton, Jr., of Brown Brothers Harriman termed it a "mild surprise" that Hudson was chosen top executive over Marley. But he added that the choice reflected the board's acknowledgement of the growing importance of international operations.[5] Hudson had been responsible for expanding AMP's operation in

Jim Marley was named chairman of the board in 1993.

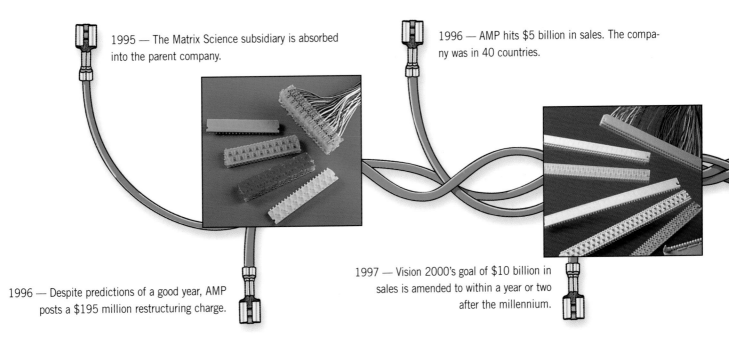

1995 — The Matrix Science subsidiary is absorbed into the parent company.

1996 — AMP hits $5 billion in sales. The company was in 40 countries.

1996 — Despite predictions of a good year, AMP posts a $195 million restructuring charge.

1997 — Vision 2000's goal of $10 billion in sales is amended to within a year or two after the millennium.

the Far East, which was an increasingly important market.

Analysts agreed that pairing Hudson and Marley was a good move.

"They work very well as a team," said Merrill Lynch analyst Jerry Labowitz, a longtime AMP follower. "I want to stress that it's a team. It is a good, natural evolutionary transformation as Mr. McInnes retires. This is the first time AMP's management is headed by a team with hands-on international experience."[6]

Another analyst, Rick Billy then with Prudential Securities, was not surprised by the moves. "The line of succession was set up two years ago when Mr. Hudson was brought back to the U.S. It makes sense. Continuity is important to AMP, and these are the two best guys running the show," he said.[7] As Marley remarked, "We have always been friends."[8]

The Challenge

AMP's reorganization was a necessary response to its customers, many of whom were firmly established multinationals with manufacturing bases around the world. According to corporate controller Bill Urkiel, the industry focus was designed to meet customers sprawling needs.

1996 AMP officers, from left: Dennis Horowitz, corporate vice president and president, The Americas; Herbert M. Cole, corporate vice president and president, AMP Asia/Pacific; Robert Ripp, corporate vice president and chief financial officer; James Marley, chairman of the board, William Hudson, president and CEO; Javad K. Hassan, corporate vice president and president, AMP GISB; and John Gurski, corporate vice president and president, AMP Global Operations, and former president of Europe, the Middle East and Africa.

"The contemporary business environment is characterized by tumultuous change, intense competition and increasingly demanding customers. For us to successfully grow in this dynamic world, we have to become more efficient by continually focusing on speed, service, quality, innovation, flexibility and cost. We must deliver creative product solutions to our customers seamlessly anywhere around the world and in the process, optimize AMP's global marketing, engineering and manufacturing resources. We must ensure that we are not duplicating our development and capital investments. To accomplish this, we are reengineering the financial processes of our company. This includes a return on asset focus through AVA

(AMP Value Added) and the introduction of auto-mated performance measurements globally by product competency, geography, and customer-defined industry."[9]

CEO Hudson had been working on a plan to reorganize AMP since 1991 when, as executive vice president, CEO McInnes gave him free reign to think about the changing business environment. In 1992, three months before he was elected CEO, Hudson gave a pivotal speech at the fist global executive leadership meeting in Munich, Germany, that forecasted his plan. In January, 1993, the globalization of AMP began.

"I came to it from a process standpoint not the organizational, structural standpoint and the process standpoint led me to say I want to develop a series of processes that allow people throughout the AMP world to reach across their boundaries and borders without concern about how their executive management may feel or not

feel and communicate and share knowledge and share practices and ideas and products without any feeling of parochial ownership getting in the way of that process."[10]

Hudson also introduced Vision 2000 in conjunction with the reorganization. As he envisioned it, Vision 2000 was more than a financial goal. There were three elements: defining AMP as a "globe-able" company, defining AMP as a growth company (which included the $10 billion goal), and regaining financial viability by striving to achieve a 20 percent return on its equity.

In June, 1994, AMP "flipped the switch" and took a series of concrete steps toward Hudson's

---

AMP's reorganization was originally structured around this 1996 business model, which divides the company's businesses into regional, product and industry focuses. This matrix, which continues to evolve, replaced the company's old "silo" hierarchy.

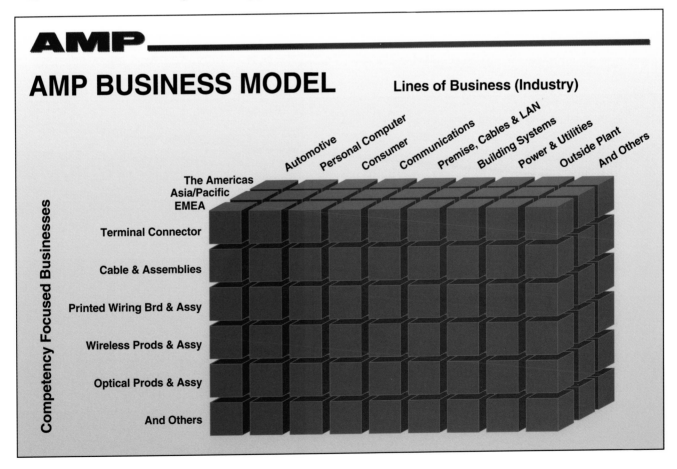

THE WHITAKER CENTER

UNCAS AENEUS WHITAKER WAS generous and caring as both employer and citizen. Marshall Holcombe, AMP's chief patent attorney and a longtime friend of Whitaker, recalled a story about his boss that dates from Whitaker's retirement in Port Royal in Naples, Florida: "I saw him out in the front of his house and asked him about giving something to the hospital and he wrote out a check right then on the hood of his car for 50,000 bucks. He was that kind of guy, but he didn't say much about it."[1]

When he died in 1975, he left hundreds of millions of dollars to the Whitaker Foundation to award contributions and grants largely in the field of biomedical engineering (a lifelong interest).[2] However, part of that money has been committed to help build the $51 million Whitaker Center for Science and the Arts, a project that will greatly enhance Harrisburg.

The Whitaker Foundation donated $7 million to the Center, according to Hal McInnes, former chairman and CEO of AMP. In 1997, McInnes served as chair of the Whitaker Center and sat on the Governing Committee of the Whitaker Foundation. "If they hadn't made a commitment of that level, the project wouldn't have gone forward," McInnes said.[3]

AMP itself, through the AMP Foundation, donated a grant of $1.5 million for the lobby area. The AMP Foundation was incorporated in 1977. It supports nonprofit groups, with a focus on education and emphasis on math and science.

"We believe the AMP Grand Lobby is the most appropriate choice for our contribution opportunity," said CEO Bill Hudson. "You go through the door of the building named for our founder, and enter the area named for the company whose growth and success have made these two significant grants possible."[4]

With funding from the public sector and corporate contributions, construction was set to be completed by 1998. The Whitaker Center's mission is to connect the local arts and theater scene with Harrisburg in a setting that is comfortable, accessible and appealing.

A Performing Arts Theater with a capacity for 600, an inter-active Science Center (which was designed with input from local grade schoolers), a 3-D IMAX theater with a 6-story screen, and space for meetings and receptions are components of the design.

goal. The first was redefining itself as a global company instead of a series of fiefdoms around the world. Next, a business model was developed that was customer-focused, as well as tightly focused on AMP's "core competencies." The third step was to "leverage all global resources more effectively through the establishment of planes of organization. One being technical, another being finance, another being global operations, which effectively glues the engineering, manufacturing practices, logistics practices and everything else together." Finally, AMP would undergo a cultural transformation.[11]

In 1993, the board elected four regional presidents: Herbert Cole in the Asia/Pacific region; John Gurski in Europe/Middle East/Africa; Javad K. Hassan in the Global Interconnect Systems Business; and Dennis Horowitz in the Americas. AMP also established its first overseas finance company in 1996. Called AMP Finance, Ltd., the division was formed to help finance programs started by the various acquisitions and joint ventures. "We had gotten into a lot more inter-company lending," noted Joseph Overbaugh, AMP treasurer.[12]

With the global organization taking shape, AMP began fine-tuning other parts of the company.

The company needed to act more like a single unit. "We started after the house was built," said Nazario Proietto, who was vice president of Southern Europe before being named a global president for the Power and Utilities Division. "We cannot change the foundation. Let's look at the

Above: The new AMP Japan plant in Shizouka, 1992. By the 1990s, AMP had a 40-year track record in Japan. The company also established an engineering center.

Below: The engineering center on Fulling Mill Road, occupied in 1995 by the Global Interconnect Systems Business, later the AMP Global Communications Business.

needs of the market on a global basis so that we can determine what the elements are to characterize this product offering in a way that satisfies Japan, that satisfies Italy, that satisfies England, that satisfies the U.S."[13]

The marketing challenge was addressed by global marketing teams. As envisioned by Ted Dalrymple, vice president of Global Marketing, teams of engineers, marketing specialists and salesmen would service one account in however many countries that customer had plants, with one contact person who was called a Global Account Manager. With Bill Hudson's blessing, Dalrymple

set up a marketing structure capable of "following our customers no matter what country they go to or what product they need."[14]

"We decided to start out slowly. The Global Account Manager in theory has quite a bit of power. The accounts should know that they have a man they can go to who is looking out for their best interests, as well as his own company. ... Somebody who understands their problems on a world basis. ... It was decided at the beginning of the program that they would live where the headquarters of the accounts were."[15]

AMP also began to worry about its information systems and uniformity around the world in terms of the flow of information. The global information system program had three basic initiatives — building worldwide networks, data warehousing, and global process reengineering using SAP. These initiatives were part of an overarching reengineering strategy to globalize AMP in support of Vision 2000.

Even as late as 1996, acceptance of information technology remained an obstacle with local managers who preferred to divert the funds to shore up local profit and loss statements. Propagation of a local access network to every professional's desktop remained a local funding decision, which stalled progress. "We were trying to build an interstate highway by getting every mayor or township supervisor to approve funding and route design," said Ron Vance, vice president and chief information officer. In response, AMP's executive team approved a $45 million investment to build the global network by 2000. In total, AMP plans to invest nearly a quarter of a billion dollars on improving and expanding its information technology capabilities in the second half of the 1990s.[16]

The engineering function was streamlined so that AMP engineers in the automotive industry worldwide could benefit from each other's work. Especially with the new research centers operation, duplication and even triplication of work was too common. Long-time engineer Linn Lightner was charged with enforcing design standards across the company so an engineer could walk into a plant in Germany and "see the same thing as in Virginia"[17] — hence the creation of the

Engineering Control Organization. Lightner, vice president of Global Engineering Management Assurance is responsible for uniformity in engineering processes and practices.

"We can't allow variations in the product that would have any effect on performance or acceptability by the customer under the same part number. That sounds like a simple thing, but it is a highly, highly complex issue because somebody producing in Malaysia needs to try to satisfy their customers and they're very likely, particularly in a place like Malaysia, producing a product that belongs to another organization. We've got 4,700

In 1992, AMP employee Kevin Smith demonstrates the fully automated IHM IDC-harness making machine developed by AMP Germany for Miele, a European appliance manufacturer.

AMP began operations in China in 1992 with the opening of AMP Shanghai, Ltd. AMP had been eyeing China for years, but delayed entry after the massacre at Tiananmen Square.

the long term product for AMP. The products that are three to five years ahead of today. ... We are going to have a structure there that somewhat parallels a business model."[19]

The Tiger's Tail

The Pacific Rim and Asia was recognized as a major growth area in the 1990s. The "Asian Miracle," as it had come to be known in the press, signified a major shift in global economics. Previously impoverished Asian and Pacific Rim countries that had once been called "Third World" earned the more promising description of "emerging nations" as their economies geared up for mass production and middle classes were created. In fact, Asian economies were some of the fastest growing in the world. Even as late as the 1980s, however, Hudson said that AMP manufacturing was primarily in Japan, while competitors were already in Singapore and Taiwan. His mission was to expand AMP across the region.

Hudson was eyeing markets in China and India and earmarking substantial funds for expansion there. Clearly, the time had arrived: Pacific Rim connector markets were growing at

engineers around the company, around the world, in 45 to 50 organizations."[18]

To accomplish this, and to get a better return on its RD&E investment, chief technology officer Phillipe Lemaitre has begun an ambitious reorganization of the research, development and engineering functions. Lemaitre started with AMP in March 1997, and immediately put his plan into action. To bring other parts of the company on board, he initiated the Technology Business Action Team, or T-BAT, which is a group of about 12 upper-level executives who have developed a series of recommendations.

Within the departments, Lemaitre has also made it a priority to develop longer term products for customers.

"What we are looking at is bringing the research center into more the domain of developing

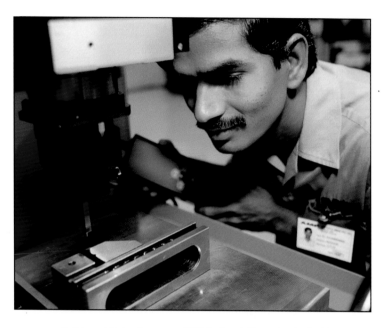

Rathinavel Rajasekaran, an AMP tool and die worker in Cochin, India, inspects a precision machine operation.

an average 12 percent per year, twice as fast as U.S. markets, and AMP was running neck-and-neck with Molex in the region.[20]

AMP approached the Chinese operation cautiously. It originally intended to open two sales and service centers there in 1989, but the Tiananmen Square massacre in June 1989 delayed negotiations between the Chinese government and foreign investors. Hudson expressed some frustration with the situation and decided to delay the opening of a Beijing office.[21]

By 1991, however, negotiations with the Chinese were complete, and AMP opened three sales offices in China. In March 1992, AMP formed a joint-venture agreement with Shanghai Electronic Components Corporation to produce connectors for the industrial and consumer markets at a plant to be built in Shanghai.[22] Also in 1991, AMP opened its first subsidiaries in India and Thailand. Further expansion in the Asia/Pacific region included a subsidiary in the Philippines opened in 1993 and sales offices in Indonesia and Vietnam in 1995-96.

AMP's expansion in this region was enhanced by its strong presence in Japan, where it had first established a subsidiary in 1957. As Japan grew into a technological power, AMP was there to supply its booming automotive and electronic industries. Then, as other Pacific Rim countries gradually developed their own electronic industries in the 1980s and 1990s, they followed the Japanese lead, copying Japanese products and using the same suppliers for components. Thus, the company found ready markets in the developing electronic industries in Korea, India, China, Southeast Asia and Malaysia.[23]

Herb Cole replaced Jean Gorjat in Asia/Pacific operations in 1995, after Gorjat retired, and has seen AMP expand across the region. "I don't think we've got a politics problem in Asia anywhere near like we have in some other countries. What we've got instead is a culture problem."[24]

J.C. Tan started in Singapore when the operation was only a couple of people and has watched it grow into three manufacturing plants and 900 people. As vice president of Asia/Pacific South, Tan looked at the late 1990s as an opportunity for even more rapid growth. "If you think in terms of the areas combined, Singapore, Philippines, Indonesia, India, Malaysia, Thailand and Vietnam the total sales is about S$350 million (Singapore dollars)," Tan said. "It's adding growth still today and in the future and from now on."[25]

David Toser, a regional controller based in Great Britain, was sent to the region in 1992 and was greatly surprised by the changes since his last trip to Japan. "When I had first gone to AMP's operations there, it was only AMP Japan and AMP Australia, and now there were a dozen or more AMP companies. There's India, Indonesia, China, and Taiwan among others ... a tremendous amount of potential amongst the Asian tigers for AMP."[26]

To handle litigation, AMP appointed and transferred a U.S. attorney to reside in Tokyo. The move was in response to a conflict. "When they have a problem in Asia/Pacific, do I need to have the attorney that's living and working there handle it or do I send somebody over there?" noted Charles Goonrey, vice president and general legal counsel. "AMP has very high standards of ethics in its global endeavors. I'm very proud to work for a company that takes the high ground."[27]

Opening the Iron Curtain

In many ways, the crumbling of the concrete Berlin Wall in 1989 was the opening act to the fall of the Soviet Union's Iron Curtain. Before the U.S.S.R. voted itself out of existence in 1991, the combined lands of the republic covered more geographic area than any other country on Earth and included East Germany, Poland, Czechoslovakia, Hungary, the Baltic States, and numerous other states.

After 1991, with communism so thoroughly discredited, countries all over the world were forced to rethink their dependence on Marxist philosophy. For companies like AMP, the end of the Cold War would signal new markets and vast opportunity for expansion.

But not at first, as former communist nations began the painful transition to a market economy. "It was a shock for us," recalled Juergen Gromer, who was area director for central Europe, an area that included many former communist countries. Gromer joined AMP in 1983 as a general manager and went on to become president of the Global Automotive Business in early 1997. "In those countries, people had no money. Business went literally from something like 50 million Deutsche marks almost down to zero. It was not possible for those people in Hungary, in Romania, or in Russia to pay for any deliveries."[28]

Peter Glaser, vice president of manufacturing for the region, remembered it this way:

"The major difficulties were certainly based in human resources because in eastern Europe, things were very much oriented to the former communist regime, and the transformation of their mood from the communist regime to free enterprise is something that takes time."[29]

AMP opened a third plant in Singapore in 1993. Part of the 'Asian Miracle,' AMP's growth rate in Singapore and throughout the Asia/Pacific region in the 1990s eclipsed the company's U.S. growth.

СОЕДИНИТЕЛЬНЫЕ

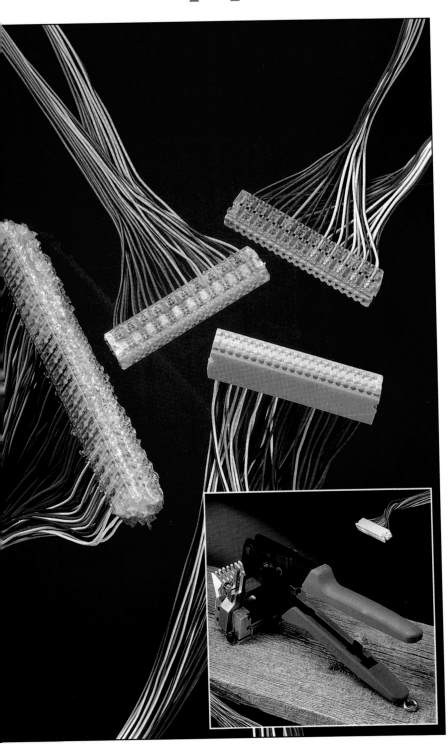

AMP moved into former Soviet countries in the 1990s, printing catalogs in a variety of languages. AMP STACK products and tools (right, below left and inset) were featured in the Russian catalogs.

This would change. In December 1992, AMP unveiled plans for a sales and manufacturing plant for high performance cable assemblies on a 20-acre site near Budapest, Hungary.[30] In 1993, it opened subsidiaries in Poznan, Poland; Brno, the Czech Republic; and Istanbul, Turkey. In 1995, subsidiaries in Tallinn, Estonia; Ljubljana, Slovenia; and sales offices in Moscow and St. Petersburg were added.[31] In 1996, sales offices in Bulgaria and Romania were brought on-line.

Sales engineers found huge differences between the former communist countries in terms of technology. The Czech Republic and Poland, for instance, were further along than Russia, where engineers were still unused to crimping technology. Rudy Eckardt, area director of Eastern Europe, was shocked to learn that his sales force had to demonstrate hand tools and "everything, because on the other side, we knew that these guys had been working for years, 20, 30, 40 years, just with very big and old-fashioned soldered connectors."[32] In fact, the Russian series of Sputnik satellites, the device that beat the United States in the race to reach space, used soldered connectors as late as 1957 — and parts of the Russian program still do.

Globability

Hudson even adopted a word for the large-scale transformation of AMP. Harold

МОДУЛИ АМП СТЭК

McInnes, provides a simple explanation for what AMP was trying to do in the 1990s:

"Looking back over the years, AMP was obviously a U.S. company. Then it became a U.S. company with 'foreign' subsidiaries. Then from there, we evolved into a multinational company, and when we saw the challenge, if you will, of getting us to address this as a 'globe-able' company, a corporation made up of many geographical companies that worked closely together like the musicians in a symphony."[33]

The primary engines behind this orchestration were Hudson and Marley. After they took over in 1993, AMP's top executives repeatedly reinforced this message in word and deed, including appointing John Gurski president of Global Operations in 1997.

A 25-year employee, Gurski started his career in operations and rose through manufacturing, gaining his overseas experience in 1992 through 1996 as president of AMP operations in Europe, the Middle East and Africa. From this vantage point, Gurski predicted the general slowdown of European Economic Union economies in the late 1990s would cause a problem for AMP. "Without new initiatives, AMP Europe would be expected to grow about 6 percent to 9 percent. If you consider that AMP's corporate objective is to grow at better than one-and-a-half times the connection device annual market growth rate forecast of 6 to 9 percent, clearly there is a gap, which is being addressed by broadening our product market and geographic scope."[34] In early 1997, Tom DiClemente replaced Gurski as head of the region.

Hudson used the term "globe-able," which was invented by Javad Hassan and Leonard Hill, to express his vision of the company's new international approach. He defined a "globe-able person" as someone with a minimum five years experience in another country and enough immersion in the culture "to know what it's like to think like someone else."[35] From almost his first day in office, Hudson held worldwide meetings to bring the company together as a team.

Teamwork across international borders was naturally realized in the AMP Export Company. In 1994, Robert Suares was challenged to set up AEC. In the AEC model, products can be drop-shipped, which means that terminals sold in South Africa will be shipped from Japan without ever physically passing through AEC in Paris. "It has the mission and the vision to fully develop and expand AMP in more than 70 countries where AMP has no base of operation whatsoever. ... We cut on costs. We save a lot of money, and we cut on lead times."[36]

A plant in Steinach, Switzerland, was opened in 1987 to bolster production in northern Europe

Highly automated AMP Modular Harness Making machines at a Citröen automobile plant in France. AMP originally had trouble penetrating the French automobile market, but by the 1990s the company was securely partnered with major French automakers.

Meanwhile, even overseas, the attitude was, "You can't sell a product on price. You must sell quality. Of course, pricing is a thing which comes to it, but first of all quality, and that was the main point. You've got to have product knowledge," noted retired Sales Manager Franz Gall, who was originally responsible for sales in Scandinavia, Germany and Benelux countries.[37] As in the United States, product knowledge translated into close liaison with the customers to determine their needs. Over a 30-year career, Benelux general sales manager Harry Kennis remarked that his job hadn't drastically changed: "It should not have to change too much because if you want to do business with a cus-

tomer, you should have a good relationship with the customer."[38]

AMP's Second Buying Spree

Throughout all of this, AMP continued its steady pace of buying companies to augment its technological expertise.

In 1993, AMP made several more acquisitions, including: Smart American Home, Elf Atochem Sensors, JWP Businessland Japan, and the Microwave Electronics Division of COM-SAT. It also made minority investments in LANart, MicroModule Systems, New Media and Wise Communications.[39]

The Connecticut-based Smart American Home was a leading sales and service organization for products used in "smart houses," which were houses "specially wired and computerized to give owners a variety of high-tech controls."[40]

Two domestic subsidiaries, Connectware and Microwave Signal, also were established in 1993.

M/A-COM products include a variety of devices for wireless voice and data transmission, including dipole antennas, power dividers and amplifiers.

Connectware focused on development of promising new ATM (Asynchronous Transfer Mode) technology for data communications, a market that analysts projected to reach more than $360 million in 1995. The Connectware unit, however, ran into trouble in 1997, when a major restructuring was announced. Facilities in Texas, North Carolina, Pennsylvania and Virginia were scheduled to be closed.

In 1994, AMP took a major step into the power utility field by acquiring Simel S.A., a France-based supplier of connectors for the worldwide power utility industry. With headquarters in Gevrey-Chambertin, near Dijon, Simel also has facilities in Canada, Spain, Germany and Great Britain and sells to customers in 60 countries. Its products include connectors for a wide range of power utility needs and railway systems, and also cable crimping and cutting tools.[41] AMP also bought ARA, a French manufacturer of automated application and harness assembly machines.

In 1995, AMP bought Akzo's share of the 50/50 joint venture, and AMP-Akzo became AMP Circuits. In mid-1997, however, with the market for additive circuit boards shrinking and a move to consolidate domestic operations underway, AMP closed the printed circuit board plant in Riverhead, New York, that had been one of AMP-Akzo's two major sites.[42]

AMP made seven acquisitions in 1996, including three domestic companies: Parm Tool, of Erie, Pennsylvania, a manufacturer of dies and molds which AMP had been using as a supplier; Madison Cable, a Massachusetts-based maker of computer cables; and Georgetown Cable, a Kentucky-based maker of cable assemblies in which AMP previously held one-half interest. In addition, AMP acquired four overseas companies: HTS, a German manufacturer of electric power connectors; Cablesa, of Brazil, maker of wire harnesses for the automotive and appliance industries; Fibernet, of Australia, providing design and installation services for

Richard Clark was chosen to head up the M/A-COM division after AMP purchased the maker of semiconductor devices and other components for the wireless communications market. AMP used M/A-COM technology to enter the wireless technology market.

premises wiring; and Ferroperm, a Danish manufacturer of electro-magnetic control devices.

M/A-COM

In 1995, AMP made by far its biggest acquisition to date, M/A-COM, the Lowell, Massachusetts-based wireless communications components firm, for an estimated $270 million in stock.

M/A-COM was founded in Boston in 1950 as Microwave Associates by four former Sylvania engineers to produce magnetrons and other microwave and radio frequency components for the military. Developing as a defense-oriented supplier, it grew rapidly and by 1985 was a *Fortune* 500 company with sales of $844 million.[43] In 1990, faced with a steep decline in defense spending, M/A-COM reorganized, shifting its focus to commercial markets.

AMP became interested in M/A-COM chiefly because of its involvement in wireless communi-

cation, a field that was growing faster than the connector market. AMP had already made an initial step in this direction when it acquired the Microwave Division of COMSAT in 1993.[44] Board members from M/A-COM and AMP began discussing a merger in 1994, and things moved swiftly from there — AMP announced the planned acquisition in early March 1995 and completed the deal in June.

Richard Clark, previously a director of corporate development for AMP, was named CEO and president of M/A-COM, as well as AMP divisional vice president. An electrical engineering graduate of the University of Pittsburgh, Clark had started with AMP in 1970 and became heavily involved with acquisitions and equity investments as they became a priority in the 1990s.[45]

Analysts concurred that AMP's commercial marketing expertise and financial clout, coupled with M/A-COM's advanced technology in an exploding field, made the merger a logical and promising move.[46]

Matrix Science

Meanwhile, business was declining for AMP's previous largest acquisition, Matrix Science, which was acquired in 1988 for $113 million to fill a gap in the military/aerospace cylindrical connectors market.

As it turned out, the timing was wrong for a military-related acquisition. Sharp cutbacks in defense spending in the early 1990s shrank the worldwide market for military connectors, and Matrix sales fell steadily, from $78 million in 1988 to about $40 million by 1994.[47] Industry journalists also speculated about a conflict in corporate culture between conservative AMP and the more "free-wheeling" and "entrepreneurial" Matrix.[48]

AMP tried several strategies to improve Matrix's performance. In 1991, it signed a deal with national distributor Hamilton/Avnet to carry Matrix connectors. It also raised prices on military connectors in 1991 (5 percent) and again in 1992 (10 percent), transferred Matrix employees to other divisions within AMP, and began developing new products for the commercial aerospace market.[49]

However, in 1995, with sales still declining, AMP folded the Matrix subsidiary and absorbed its product line within the company's Federal Systems Division.[50]

In fall 1995, AMP closed operations at the former Matrix plant near Torrance, California, moving operations to a Mount Joy, Pennsylvania plant. In January 1997, as part of a company-wide restructuring plan which included "significant cuts" in its cylindrical connector line, it transferred 200 workers at the Mount Joy plant and also closed a cylindrical connector plant in Montclair, California.[51]

New Day Dawning

In 1996 and 1997, AMP put the final parts of its plan into effect: leveraging AMP's resources better on a global basis and the cultural transformation. Hudson and Marley were moving the company from a "silo" kind of hierarchy with isolated pockets to a matrix organization where highly effective business teams cut across boundaries. "It has wreaked a lot of havoc in the company," said Richard Skaare, AMP's corporate communications executive. "And I don't think that is wrong. Under the new model people are encouraged to come out of their silos."[52]

Throughout late 1996 and 1997, the entire company was reorganized around five industry-focused groups, which complemented the existing global units. Each new industry business unit was headed by a newly minted president. The structure combined most of AMP's varied functions, marketing, sales, engineers, etc., into global divisions, including: power and utilities, headed by Nazario Proietto; personal computers, under Rudolf Gassner; automotive, under Juergen Gromer; and communications, which was an evolution and expansion of the Global Interconnect Systems Business, under Javad K. Hassan.

The final industry focus was organized by Robert Ripp in August 1997. It included the appliance industry, consumer electronics, aerospace, defense and industrial. The unit, named the Global Consumer and Industrial Division, attracts between $1.2 and $1.6 billion in sales and, according to Ripp, "represents the original core of AMP business."[53]

The benefits of the reorganization, said Hudson, are varied.

"The principal advantage is to be able to leverage our resources serving those industries more effectively on a global basis. Our customers want to be able to work with a single point, and they want to deal with a president. We're aligning the business engine to the industries we serve. For instance, in the automotive marketplace, we basically have a three-year cycle from the time one of our customers defines a new platform to the time it goes into full production. In consumer and personal computers, there is a six-month cycle from definition to full tooling. You've got to build the dynamics of your support capability and your interface capability to meet the dynamics of your industry requirement. The communication business is now based on a holistic, what I call technology, thread. That's the multimedia, broadband width technology spread from the equipment side all the way to the end users."[54]

Dr. Leonard Hill, vice president of succession and global reorganization, worked closely with CEO Hudson to manage this massive shift, in which reporting lines all changed at once and people were asked to reorder their thinking. "The opportunity and the promise are probably the greatest in the history of the company," Hill said.[55]

Besides adjusting AMP's profile to do business in a global community, this reorganization will have another profound effect on the company. By targeting new markets and introducing new products, AMP has expanded its potential market from $27 billion to $97 billion. Much of this new potential market is concentrated in the communications industries, which fall under Hassan's jurisdiction.[56]

The Business Picture

Sales were relatively flat between 1990 and 1993, rising from $3.04 billion to $3.45 billion during that period and averaging only about a 3 percent increase per year (except for 1992, at 8 percent). The next two years, 1994 and 1995, saw exceptional growth rates of 17 and 20 percent, with total sales climbing to a record $5.23 billion in 1995 and earnings per share to $1.96.[57]

Based on this trend, analysts agreed with AMP's predictions of another very good year in 1996, with earnings expected to rise to around

$2.40 per share. However, a slowdown in demand from the personal computer and cellular telephone markets, along with excess inventory and continued price erosion, again flattened sales. For the year, sales increased just 7 percent, to $5.47 billion, while earnings plummeted to $1.31 per share, which resulted in a dip in stock prices.[58] A large portion of the earnings decline was the result of a $195 million restructuring and other one-time charges to eliminate underperforming assets. The charge, which was the largest in company history, was announced in the fourth quarter of 1996 to pay for the closing of several domestic plants and for laying off up to 1,000 employees.[59]

In response to the disappointing 1996 results, four of AMP's top executives — Hudson, Marley, Hassan and president of the Americas Dennis Horowitz — received no performance-based bonuses. Horowitz left AMP in early 1997, citing "personal reasons." AMP leader Jim Marley assumed Horowitz's responsibilities in the Americas, in addition to his own duties as chairman of the board.

According to Bill Oakland, former director of investor relations, the move to tie the top executives' salary in with performance was very popular among investors. "Our management is very motivated to produce better results," Oakland said.[60]

But by 1996, AMP's future could never be jeopardized by a one-year downturn in business. The company operated subsidiaries in 40 countries, employed 45,000 people, and controlled nearly 20 percent of the global market for connectors and related devices.[61] In addition, it had 50,000 automatic machines, millions of tools in the field, and a vast catalog of connectors, splices, cable and panel assemblies, networking units, sensors, switches, electro- and fiber-optic devices and touch screen data entry systems.[62]

Below: The main auditorium of the Global Executive Leadership Center, in Harrisburg, seats several hundred and features state-of-the-art video, audio and data links around the world. The center was opened in 1995 as part of AMP's thrust to bring the company together under one global umbrella.

Right: The Global Executive Leadership Center flies flags from every country that AMP has operations in. The flag displays are designed to show that AMP's global organization doesn't belong to any single country.

AMP — A $10 Billion Small Company

All this happened in a relatively short time. AMP's first public offering, at $16.25 per share, in 1956, had heralded the growth of a quiet giant in the electronics industry. By 1997, that original share of stock would have evolved into a small portfolio of 112.32 shares.[63] In addition, AMP stock dividends have increased for 44 consecutive years.

As AMP heads toward the future, its leaders are keeping their eyes on Vision 2000. Under its guidelines, AMP would reach $10 billion in sales around the turn of the millennium. But U.A. Whitaker's legacy will not be lost — as the company climbs up the *Fortune* 500 list, its officers are steadily trying to recreate Whitaker's

dream factory of 200 people where he would "know every one of them by their first name." These words invoke the foundation of AMP's culture and AMP's belief in people. Speaking of his own legacy and AMP's future, Hudson, CEO and president, said:

"My ultimate contribution is obviously when all this is really working successfully and this company is reaching Vision 2000, but probably more importantly, that there's a Vision 2010 and 2020 going forward, to keep it going. The other thing I think I'm trying to do is fight 'bigitis,' and to get these pockets of resistance out of this company so that we feel like a small company and can act like a small company, and yet have a large revenue and earnings base."[64]

Notes to Sources

Chapter One

1. U.A. Whitaker, Report on Industrial Manufacturers, submitted to Booz, Fry, Allen and Hamilton. August, 12, 1941, p. 28.
2. William Cohn, *The End is Just the Beginning: U.A. Whitaker, Biography of an Engineer*, (Pittsburgh: Carnegie-Mellon, 1980), p. 118.
3. *Ibid.*, pp.10–16.
4. *Ibid.*, p. 15.
5. *Ibid.*, p. 19.
6. *Ibid.*, p. 30.
7. *Ibid.*, pp. 46–47.
8. *Ibid.*, pp. 82–83.
9. Leon Whipple, *A U.A. Whitaker Characteristic*, unpublished manuscript, undated, p. 1.
10. William Lane, interviewed by Alex Lieber, May 7, 1997. Transcript, p. 2.
11. Cohn, p. 99.
12. Whitaker report, pp. 6–7.
13. Bern Sharfman, *The AMP Story: Right Connections*, (AMP corporate history, 1991), p. 8.
14. Whitaker report, p. 2.
15. *Ibid.*, p. 3.
16. *Ibid.*
17. Cohn, p. 130.
18. Whitaker report, p. 13.
19. *Ibid.*, p. 19.
20. *Ibid.*, p. 14.
21. *Ibid.*, p. 4.
22. *Ibid.*, p. 11.
23. Sharfman, p. 9.
24. John B. Rae, *Climb to Greatness: The American Aircraft Industry, 1920-1960*, (Cambridge, Mass: MIT Press, 1968), pp. 152, 169.
25. F.O. Stebbins and L.A. Taylor, "Electric Connections on Aircraft," *Electrical Engineering*, (Vol. 63, Dec. 1944), p. 906-911.
26. Cohn, p. 113.
27. F.H. Wells, and J.C. Balsbaugh, "Solderless Terminals," *Electrical Engineering*, (Vol. 63, Dec. 1944), pp. 933-938.
28. A–MP catalog, Bulletin 11, 1941.
29. Cohn, p. 114.
30. Rae, p. 61.
31. Cohn, p. 109.
32. Whitaker report, pp. 13–14.
33. *Ibid.*, p. 21.
34. *Ibid.*, p. 23.
35. *Ibid.*, p. 24.
36. *Ibid.*, p. 26.
37. *Ibid.*, p. 28.
38. Cohn, p. 119.
39. *Ibid.*, p. 121.
40. Cohn, p. 123.
41. Sharfman, pp. 10–11.
42. Al Curtis, interviewed by Bern Sharfman, January, 1988. Transcript, p. 2.

Chapter Two

1. Tom Freedom, interviewed by Sel Friedlander, August 7,1996. Transcript, p. 21.
2. William Cohn, *The End is Just the Beginning: U.A. Whitaker, Biography of an Engineer*, (Pittsburgh: Carnegie-Mellon, 1980), p. 124.
3. *Ibid.*, p. 8.
4. *Ibid.*, p. 128.
5. *Ibid.*, p. 136.
6. Bern Sharfman, *The AMP Story: Right Connections*, (AMP corporate history, 1991), p. 41.
7. Cohn, p. 131.
8. *Ibid.*
9. Leon Whipple, *A U.A. Whitaker Characteristic*, unpublished manuscript, undated.
10. Cohn, p. 131.
11. *Ibid.*, pp. 146–147.
12. Ken Neijstrom, interviewed by Sel Friedlander, April, 18, 1996. Transcript, p. 4.
13. Cleve Fredricksen, interviewed by Bern Sharfman, December 3, 1987. Transcript, p. 3.
14. Cohn, p. 149.
15. *The Harrisburg Story*, (AMP internal history, published during the 1950s), pp. 5, 10.
16. Tom Freedom, interviewed by Sel Friedlander, August 7, 1996. Transcript, p. 21.
17. *A–MP Solderless Wiring Devices*, company catalog, 1943, sec. 20, p. 2003.
18. Neijstrom interview, p. 10.
19. Sharfman, pp. 19–20.
20. Freedom interview, p. 7.
21. Cohn, p. 135.
22. *Ibid.*, p. 150.
23. *Ibid.*, p. 144
24. *Ibid.*, p. 152.

25. *Ibid.*, pp. 153–54.
26. *International Directory of Company Histories*, editor Paula Kepos, (St. James Press, 1996), Vol. 11, p. 515.
27. Cohn, pp. 157, 162.
28. John B. Rae, *Climb to Greatness: The American Aircraft Industry*, 1920-1960, (Cambridge, Mass: MIT Press, 1968), pp. 116–17.
29. Cohn, pp. 150, 162.
30. Neijstrom interview, p. 8.
31. Cohn, 168.
32. Sharfman, pp. 23-24; Cohn, pp. 168–69.
33. "$75,000 Blaze Destroys Glen Rock Defense Plant," *York Gazette and Daily*, May 22, 1943.
34. Al Curtis, interviewed by Bern Sharfman, January, 1988. Transcript, p. 18.
35. Leon Whipple, interviewed by Sel Friedlander, April 18, 1996. Transcript, p. 5.
36. Sharfman, pp. 24-26; Cohn, p. 170.
37. Whipple, interviewed by Sel Friedlander, April 18, 1996. Transcript, pp. 3-4.
38. Barton, Michael, *Life by the Moving Road*, "The History of AMP," article by Mark Dorfman, (Woodland Hills, CA: Windsor), 1983, p. 3.
39. Cohn, p. 171.
40. Neijstrom interview, p. 12.
41. Cohn, p. 179.
42. *Ibid.*, pp. 174–176.
43. *Ibid.*, p. 167.

Chapter Two Sidebar

1. Harold Mansfield, *Vision: A Saga of the Sky*, (New York: Duell, Sloan and Pearce), 1956, p. 173.
2. John B. Rae, *Climb To Greatness: The American Aircraft Industry*, 1920-1960, (Cambridge, MA: MIT Press, 1968), p. 117.

Chapter Three

1. Joseph Brenner, interviewed by Sel Friedlander, December 14, 1987. Transcript, p. 5.
2. Cleve Fredricksen, interviewed by Bern Sharfman, December 3, 1987. Transcript, p. 17.
3. AMP board minutes, Vol. 4, June 6, 46.
4. Bill Oakland, interviewed by Jon VanZile, August 7, 1997.
5. William Cohn, *The End is Just the Beginning: U.A. Whitaker, Biography of an Engineer*, (Pittsburgh: Carnegie-Mellon, 1980), p. 191.
6. Tom Freedom, interviewed by Sel Friedlander, September 28, 1996. Videotaped.
7. AMP board minutes, March 1, 1944, April 14, 1949; and Cohn, p. 193.
8. *Ibid.*, p. 193.
9. *Ibid.*
10. William Cohn, unpublished manuscript written for AMP's 40th anniversary, pp. 3–13.
11. Chet Timmins, interviewed by Sel Friedlander, February 27, 1997. Transcript, p. 2.
12. Cohn, 40th, pp. 3-13.
13. *Ibid.*, p. 187.
14. Joseph Brenner, interviewed by Sel Friedlander, October 1, 1996. Videotaped.
15. Cohn, biography, p. 198.
16. Brenner interview.
17. *Ibid.*
18. Tom Freedom, interviewed by Sel Friedlander, August 7, 1996. Videotaped.
19. Webster's New World Encyclopedia, (New York: Prentice Hall, 1992), pp. 261.
20. Cohn, biography, p. 194.
21. Brenner interview.
22. *Ibid.*
23. Bern Sharfman, *The AMP Story: Right Connections*, (AMP corporate history, 1991), p. 59.
24. Cohn, biography, pp. 184, 196.
25. Sharfman, p. 66.
26. Dottie Yingling, interviewed by Sel Friedlander, May 10, 1996. Transcript, page 7.
27. Freedom interview.
28. Sharfman, p. 61.
29. Sel Friedlander, interviewed by the author, September 19, 1996.
30. Sharfman, pp. 68–70; and Cohn, biography, p. 210.
31. Cohn, biography, p. 202.

Chapter Four

1. Dottie Yingling, interviewed by Sel Friedlander, May 10, 1996. Transcript, page 16.
2. William Cohn, unpublished manuscript written for

AMP's 40th anniversary, chap. 4, p. 1.

3. *Ibid.*

4. Harold G. Vatter, *The U.S. Economy in the 1950s*, (Westport, Connecticut: Greenwood Press, 1963), p. 11.

5. *Ibid.*, p. 175.

6. *Ibid.*, p. 74.

7. William Cohn, *The End is Just the Beginning: U.A. Whitaker, Biography of an Engineer*, (Pittsburgh: Carnegie-Mellon, 1980), p. 7.

8. Gordon Drane, interviewed by Sel Friedlander, July 26, 1996. Transcript, p. 5.

9. Yingling interview, p. 16.

10. FASTON file, patent binder, provided by Linn Lightner.

11. Automatic Machine Division, Annual Report 1951.

12. Automatic Machine Division, Annual Report 1952.

13. Cohn, biography, p. 210.

14. *IBM: A Special Company*, IBM corporate history, p. 36.

15. Vatter, p. 168.

16. Automatic Machine Division, Annual Report 1951, p. 8.

17. Correspondence from I.S. Homans to U.A. Whitaker, July, 10, 1950.

18. Correspondence from U.A. Whitaker to I.S. Homans, July 26, 1950.

19. Automatic Machine Division, Annual Report, 1952, p. 2.

20. Cohn, biography, p. 210.

21. Correspondence from R.C. Campbell to G. Earle Walker, July 30, 1951.

22. Correspondence from Whitaker to Cleve Fredricksen, November 6, 1951.

23. Ken Neijstrom, interviewed by Sel Friedlander, April, 18, 1996. Transcript, p. 23.

24. S. Wilson Pollock, interviewed by Sel Friedlander, September 20, 1996. Transcript, p. 4.

25. Bern Sharfman, *The AMP Story: Right Connections*, (AMP corporate history, 1991), p. 81.

26. Cohn, biography, p. 212.

27. Correspondence from R.C. Campbell to S. Wilson Pollock, October 1, 1952.

28. Daniel Burnand, interviewed by Sel Friedlander, October 17, 1996. Transcript, p. 1.

29. Cohn, biography, pp. 220–221.

30. Sharfman, p. 81.

31. Correspondence from Bill Pollock to U.A. Whitaker, March 18, 1955.

32. *Ibid.*

33. *Ibid.*

34. Cohn, biography, p. 222.

35. Cohn, biography, p. 213.

36. Tom Freedom, interviewed by Sel Friedlander, October 10, 1996.

37. Correspondence from G. Earle Walker to Oliver Holmes, April 22, 1953.

38. Internal Correspondence, May 8, 1951.

39. A–MP board minutes, October 23, 1952, Vol. 5, p. 152.

40. Sharfman, p. 102.

41. Correspondence from Walker to Holmes, December 8, 1952.

42. *Ibid.*

43. Sharfman, pp. 102–103.

Chapter Five

1. Correspondance from Marshall Holcombe to U.A. Whitaker, October 15, 1956.

2. *Ibid.*

3. AMP board minutes, October 5, 1956, Vol. 8, p. 48.

4. William Lange, interviewed by Bern Sharfman, October 26, 1997. Transcript, p. 35.

5. William Cohn, *The End is Just the Beginning: U.A. Whitaker, Biography of an Engineer*, (Pittsburgh: Carnegie-Mellon), p. 11.

6. *Ibid.*, p. 13.

7. Planning Committee minutes, October 20, 1959.

8. Harold G. Vatter, *The U.S. Economy in the 1950s*, (Westport, Connecticut: Greenwood Press, 1963), pp. 205–6.

9. Cohn, biography, p. 230.

10. Operating Committee minutes, September 25, 1956.

11. Cohn, biography, p. 230.

12. Sarnoff, David. "Electronics Revolution, Present and Future," *New York Times Magazine*, Sept., 30, 1956, p. 14.

13. 1956 AMP Annual Report, p. 3.

14. Product Group Summary Study, General Products Division, October 18, 1957.

15. Vittorio Pozzi, interviewed by Sel Friedlander, October 18, 1996. Transcript, p. 11.

16. William Cohn, unpublished manuscript written for AMP's 40th anniversary, p. 4.

17. AMP 1956 *Catalog of Terminals and Connectors applied with Automatic Machines*, p. 16.

18. Memo from G. Earle Walker to Dottie Yingling, September 18, 1958.

19. Cohn, 40th, p. 7.

20. Correspondence from Marshall Holcombe to U.A. Whitaker, October 15, 1956. AMP General Correspondence, 1957.

21. Correspondence from Edward Newberger to U.A. Whitaker, March 5, 1957. AMP General Correspondence, 1957.

22. Burt Hendricks to Edward Newberger, March 11, 1957. AMP General Correspondence, 1957.

23. AMP 1956 Annual Report, p. 7; and Cohn, biography, p. 231.

24. AMP 1959 Annual Report, p. 9; and Joe Sweeney, interviewed by Sel Friedlander, November 5, 1996. Videotaped.

25. William Cohn, unpublished manuscript written for AMP's 40th anniversary, p. 22.

26. William Cohn, *The End is Just the Beginning: U.A. Whitaker, Biography of an Engineer*, (Pittsburgh: Carnegie-Mellon), p. 209.

27. General Products Performance Report, 1955; C&D Division Annual Report, 1956.

28. AMP General Products Division, 1956 Annual Report, p. 16.

29. AMP 1956 Annual Report, p. 6.

30. AMP General Products Division, 1957 Annual Report, p. 18.

31. Memo to AMP office employees, November 1, 1955.

32. AMP General Products Division, 1956 Annual Report, p. 18.

33. Correspondence from Leon Whipple to U.A. Whitaker, April 5, 1956.

34. Memo from Leon Whipple to U.A. Whitaker, December 31, 1958.

35. *Ibid.*

36. Sharfman, p. 174.

37. Cohn, 40th, p. 14.

38. William Lange, interviewed by Bern Sharfman, October 26, 1987.

39. Bud Howell, interviewed by Sel Friedlander, February 9, 1997. Transcript, p. 17.

40. Russ Knerr, interviewed by Sel Friedlander, August 23, 1988. Transcript, p. 13.

41. Planning Committee minutes, July 14, 1959.

42. Bill Oakland, interviewed by Jeff Rodengen, December 9, 1996. Transcript, p. 9.

43. Cohn, 40th, pp. 9–10.

Chapter Six

1. Leon Whipple, interviewed by Sel Friedlander, April 18, 1996. Transcript, p. 9.

2. Alex Groner, *The American Heritage History of American Business & Industry*, (New York, American Heritage, 1972), p. 351.

3. *Ibid.*

4. AMP Annual Reports, 1960 and 1969.

5. Groner, p. 354.

6. Groner, p. 355.

7. Joe Sweeney, interviewed by Sel Friedlander, November 5, 1996. Videotaped.

8. *Ibid.*

9. *Ibid.*

10. Homer Henschen, interviewed by Sel Friedlander, November 26, 1996. Videotaped.

11. *Ibid.*

12. *Ibid.*

13. *Ibid.*

14. Bill Narigan, interviewed by Sel Friedlander, May 23, 1996. Transcript, p. 6.

15. Henschen interview.

16. Joe Brenner, interviewed by Sel Friedlander, October 1, 1996.

17. Henschen interview.

18. Don Shoemaker, interviewed by Sel Friedlander, December 11, 1996. Transcript, p. 4.

19. Henschen interview.

20. Bill Hildebrand, interviewed by Sel Friedlander, December 11, 1996. Transcript, p. 8.

21. AMP 1968 Annual Report, p. 14.

22. AMP 1961 Annual Report, p. 5.

23. William Cohn, unpublished manuscript written for AMP's 40th anniversary, p. 10.

24. *The New York Times*, February 25, 1965, p. 45.
25. Whipple interview, p. 9.
26. Linn Lightner, interviewed by Sel Friedlander, December 6, 1996.
27. AMP 1964 Annual Report, p. 10.
28. Lightner interview.
29. Planning Committee minutes, June 20, 1966.
30. Planning Committee minutes, January 15, 1968.
31. Jerome Lyman, *Electronics Products*, August 21, 1972, p. 28–35.
32. Lightner interview.
33. Sweeney interview; AMP 1963 Annual Report, p. 8.
34. AMP 1963 Annual Report, p. 11.
35. Sweeney interview.
36. Dimitry Grabbe, interviewed by Sel Friedlander, January 15, 1997. Transcript, p. 12.
37. *The New York Times*, April 12, 1969, p. 45.
38. *Ibid.*
39. Heritage Room display.
40. James Marley, interviewed by Sel Friedlander, February 4, 1997. Transcript, p. 4.
41. Bill Broske, interviewed by Sel Friedlander, December 12, 1996. Transcript, p. 18.
42. Bern Sharfman, *The AMP Story: Right Connections*, (AMP Corporate History, 1991), p. 48.
43. AMP 1965 Annual Report, p. 7.
44. *Electrical World*, Sept. 8, 1969.
45. Cohn, 40th, Chp. 5, p. 16.
46. Cohn, 40th, Chp. 5, p. 18.

47. John Hopkins, interviewed by Sel Friedlander, Transcript, page 5.
48. Whipple interview, March 25, 1996.
49. Sharfman, p. 90.
50. AMP 1960 Annual Report, p. 7.
51. AMP Heritage Room.
52. Operating Committee minutes, May 10, 1960.
53. AMP 1963 Annual Report, p. 5.
54. AMP 1966 Annual Report, p. 5.
55. Operating Committee minutes, October 10, 1961.
56. AMP 1964 Annual Report, 1967 Annual Report.
57. Richard Stuart-Prince, interviewed by Sel Friedlander, October 11, 1996. Transcript, page 3.

Chapter Six Sidebar

1. Tom Freedom, interviewed by Sel Friedlander, August 7, 1996.
2. William Cohn, *The End is Just the Beginning: U.A. Whitaker, Biography of an Engineer*, (Pittsburgh: Carnegie-Mellon, 1980), p. 69, 201.
3. *Ibid.*, p. 200.
4. *Ibid.*, pp. 198–200.
5. *Ibid.*, p. 201.
6. William Lange, interviewed by Bern Sharfman, October 26, 1987. Transcript, p. 37.
7. *Ibid.*, p. 5.
8. Homer Henschen, interviewed by Sel Friedlander, November 26, 1996.

9. Marshall Holcombe, interviewed by Sel Frieldander, February 9, 1997. Transcript, p. 4.
10. Leon Whipple, interviewed by Sel Friedlander, March 25, 1996.
11. The Whitaker Foundation pamphlet.
12. Burt Hendricks, interviewed by Sel Friedlander, January 7, 1996.

Chapter Seven

1. William Cohn, unpublished manuscript written for AMP's 40th anniversary, Chp. 7, pg. 2.
2. AMP 1971 Annual Report, p. 3.
3. McCrone, Dick. *Sunday Patriot News*. Jan. 10, 1971.
4. Howard Peiffer, interviewed by author, February 10, 1997. Transcript, p. 9.
5. Cohn, 40th, Ch. 7, pg. 2.
6. *Electronic Design News*, Dec. 20, 1973, p. 18.
7. *Ibid.*, p. 18.
8. *Ibid.*, p. 22.
9. Cohn, 40th, Ch. 7, pg. 5.
10. *Electronic Business*, April 1978, p. 20.
11. AMP 1977 Annual Report, p. 18.
12. *Computer Design*, March 1978, p. 38.
13. Dave Rundle, interviewed by Jon Rounds, December 19, 1996. Taped.
14. Correspondence from M. Cronin to W.J. Keating, Oct. 22, 1970.
15. Correspondence from M. Cronin to W.J. Keating,

Nov. 9, 1970; and F.W. Raring to John Adams, Feb. 11, 1971.

16. Memo from Jay L. Seitchik, May 3, 1972.

17. Rundle interview.

18. *Ibid.*

19. *Ibid.*

20. Linn Lightner, interviewed by Sel Friedlander, December 12, 1996.

21. Cohn 40th, Chp. 6, p. 18.

22. *Ibid.*, Chp. 7, p. 13.

23. *Ibid.*, Chp 6, p. 18.

24. *Ibid.*, Chp. 6, p. 19.

25. Schneiderman, Ron. *Electronic News*, May 29, 1972, p. 17.

26. Cohn 40th, Chp. 6, p. 21.

27. AMP 1978 Annual Report, p. 6.

28. King, James. *Financial Post*, June 8, 1974.

29. *Electronic News*, Oct. 21, 1974.

30. AMP 1979 Annual Report, p. 3.

31. Dennis Morse, interviewed by Sel Friedlander, October 10, 1996. Transcript, p. 3.

32. Gerry Schmidt, interviewed by Sel Friedlander, October 14, 1996. Transcript, p. 9.

33. Planning Committee minutes, 1970 and 1973.

34. Operating Committee minutes, June 13, 1961.

35. Jean Gorjat, interviewed by Sel Friedlander, January 7, 1996. Transcript, p. 26.

36. Bob Nishiyama, interviewed by Sel Friedlander, April 10, 1997. Transcript, p. 4.

37. *Ibid.*, p. 2.

38. *Ibid.*, p. 10.

39. Dominique Chavin, interviewed by Sel Friedlander, January 15, 1997. Transcript, p. 6.

40. George Tsygalnitzky, interviewed by Sel Friedlander, October 18, 1996. Transcript, p. 8.

41. AMP Annual Reports, 1970 through 1974.

42. Cohn, 40th, Chp. 7, p. 3.

43. *Forbes*, Jan.1, 1976, p. 148.

44. AMP 1974 Annual Report, p. 5.

45. Cohn, William, *The End is Just the Beginning: U.A. Whitaker, Biography of an Engineer*, (Pittsburgh: Carnegie-Mellon, 1980), p. 272.

46. *Ibid.*

47. AMP 1975 Annual Report, p. 3.

48. Joe Brenner, interviewed by Sel Friedlander, September 6, 1996.

49. Chet Timmins, interviewed by Sel Friedlander, February 27, 1997. Transcript, p. 7.

50. AMP Press Release, May 4, 1979.

51. AMP Annual Report 1972, and AMP Annual Report 1979.

52. AMP Press release, May 4, 1979.

53. *Ward's Automotive Reports*, Sept. 16, 1974.

54. *Electronic News*, Oct. 15, 1979, p. 1.

55. AMP 1966 Annual Report, and *Wall Street Journal*, May 13, 1968.

56. *Electronic News*, Oct. 15, 1979, p. 4.

57. *Business Week*, June 27, 1977.

58. *Business Week*, July 2, 1979, p.53.

Chapter Eight

1. Kindel, Stephen, "Ample Rewards," *Financial World*, June 14, 1988, p. 23.

2. *The Wall Street Journal*, May 14, 1984.

3. Sharfman, Bern. *The AMP Story: Right Connections*, (AMP corporate history, 1991), pp. 190-191.

4. "AMP's Raab is Elected Chief, Succeeds Brenner," *The Wall Street Journal*, April 23, 1982.

5. AMP press release, July 27, 1983.

6. Saporito, Bill, "Companies That Compete Best," *Fortune*, May 22, 1989, p. 40.

7. Kindel, Stephen, "Ample Rewards," *Financial World*, June 14, 1988, p. 23.

8. Bertrand, Kate, "The Just-in-Time Mandate," *Business Marketing*, November 1986, p. 45.

9. *Ibid.*, p. 46.

10. Kindel, p. 23.

11. Sharfman, p. 127.

12. *Ibid.*, p. 96.

13. Kindel, p. 23.

14. Sharfman, p. 118.

15. Lorincz, James A., "Getting Quality–Connected at AMP," *Purchasing World*, August 1985, p. 31.

16. Saporito, p. 40.
17. *Ibid.*
18. AMP 1989 Annual Report, p. 5.
19. "Connectors Today," *Electronic Buyers' News*, Feb. 24, 1986, p. T–5.
20. Walter Raab, interviewed by Bern Sharfman, December 20, 1988. Transcript, p.16.
21. "AMP to Acquire Concern in Texas for $300 million," *The Wall Street Journal*, Nov. 24, 1980; AMP 1980 Annual Report, p. 3.
22. Sonenclar, Robert J. "AMP To Buy Switch Line," *Electronic Buyers' News*, April 20, 1981.
23. *Ibid.*
24. *Ibid.*
25. "AMP Sues Chomerics Over Keyboards," *Electronic Buyers' News*, June 27, 1983.
26. "Grace to Buy Chomerics in $99M Stock Swap," *Electronic News*, March 11, 1985.
27. Vinton, Bob. "AMP to Exit Full–Travel Membranes," *Electronic News*, Sept. 2, 1985.
28. *Ibid.*
29. AMP 1989 Annual Report, p. 3.
30. Carroll Touch news release, July 27, 1983.
31. Mitchell, Russell. "A Touch of Competition in Touch Screen Technology," *Electronic Business*, March 1, 1985.
32. *Ibid.*
33. AMP 1985 Annual Report, p. 9.

34. AMP 1989 Annual Report, p. 3.
35. Rothschild, K. "Manufacturers Invest Heavily in Fiber Optics," *Electronic News*, Nov. 18, 1985.
36. Sharfman, p. 130.
37. Ben Conner, interviewed by Sel Friedlander, May 28, 1996. Transcript, p. 5.
38. Sharfman, p. 131.
39. "Off the Shelf," *Electronic News*, Feb. 2, 1981.
40. AMP 1983 Annual Report, p. 16.
41. Sharfman, p. 131.
42. AMP 1984 Annual Report, p. 17.
43. AMP 1985 Annual Report, and AMP 1988 Annual Report.
44. AMP 1987 Annual Report, p. 9.
45. Sharfman, p. 132.
46. "Connectors Today," *Electronic Buyers' News*, Feb. 24, 1986, p. T–10.
47. David Henschel, interviewed by the author, February 10, 1997. Transcript, p. 6.
48. AMP 1982 Annual Report.
49. AMP 1983 Annual Report, and AMP 1984 Annual Report.
50. McAdoo, Maisie, "Full User Shelves Cut Parts Sales," *Electronic Buyers' News*, July 30, 1984.
51. McInnes, Harold, "Forecast 1986," *Electri–onics*, Dec. 1985, pp. 16–17.
52. Kindel, Stephen, "Ample Rewards," *Financial World*, June 14, 1988, p. 24.

53. Smith, Randall, "Computer Makers Find Slump Hard to Take," *The Wall Street Journal*, Oct. 10, 1985.
54. Harold McInnes, interviewed by Sel Friedlander, May 2, 1996. Transcript, p 8.
55. "Winner Take All," edited Bryce Webster, (New York: American Management Association), 1987.
56. AMP 1985 Annual Report, p. 1.
57. AMP 1985 Annual Report, p. 8.
58. Jackson, Tony, "Wired for the Future," *Financial Times*, May 15, 1996.
59. Merrill Yohe, interviewed by author, February 10, 1997. Transcript, p. 12.
60. Phil Guarneschelli, interviewed by Sel Friedlander, November 15, 1996. Transcript, p. 4.
61. Cohn, William, *The End is Just the Beginning: U.A. Whitaker, Biography of an Engineer,* (Pittsburgh: Carnegie-Mellon, 1980), p. 170.
62. "Connector Outlook Rosy," *Electronic Buyers' News*, Oct. 20, 1980.
63. Kindel, p. 24.
64. International Directory of Company Histories, ed. Tina Grant, 1996, Vol. 11, p. 27.
65. *The Fleck Report on the Connector Industry*, Fleck Telesis Inc., Vol. V, No. 6, June 1988, p. 4.
66. Burns, Matthew, "AMP, Molex Court Matrix," *Electronic Buyers' News*,

Nov. 9, 1987; and "AMP, Molex Up Matrix Stakes," *Electronic Buyers' News*, Nov. 16, 1987.

67. "Hear 3M Will Join Bidding for Matrix," *Electronic Buyers' News*, Nov. 16, 1987.

68. *The Fleck Report on the Connector Industry,* Fleck Telesis Inc., Vol. V, No. 6, June 1988.

69. AMP 1988 Annual Report, p. 2.

70. Fleck, p. 2.

71. AMP 1988 Annual Report, p. 2

72. McInnes interview, p. 7.

73. *Ibid.*

74. AMP Annual Reports, 1984, 1987, 1989.

75. AMP Annual Reports, 1980-89.

76. Gerry Schmidt, interviewed by Sel Friedlander, Oct. 14, 1996. Transcript, p. 11.

77. Alfred Greger, interviewed by Sel Friedlander, October 14, 1996. Transcript, pp. 6-7.

78. Bill Hudson, interviewed by Jon VanZile, August 7, 1997. Taped.

79. AMP 1986 Annual Report, p. 2.

80. "AMP Advances With Customer-First Stance in Production, Marketing," *Business International*, Aug. 2, 1985.

81. Lappen, Alyssa A., "Worldwide Connections," *Forbes*, June 27, 1988, p. 80.

82. Kindel, p. 23.

83. Lappen, p. 80.

84. AMP 1984 Annual Report, p. 9.

85. Oakland interview.

86. AMP 1984 Annual Report, p. 9.

87. Carol Ritter, interviewed by author, February 12, 1997. Transcript, p. 3.

88. John Kegel, interviewed by author, February 12, 1997. Transcript, p. 10.

89. Phil Guarneschelli, interviewed by the author, February, 11, 1997. Transcript, p. 2.

Chapter Nine

1. *Connection Technology*, November 1990, p. 17.

2. AMP 1990 Annual Report, p. 2.

3. "Executive Comment: Decade of the 1990s — The Game Gets Tougher," *Connection Technology*, November 1990.

4. *Ibid.*

5. Dean Hooper, interviewed by author, February 12, 1997. Transcript, p. 19.

6. Bill Narigan, interviewed by Sel Friedlander, May 23, 1996. Transcript, page 27.

7. Jasinowski, Jerry and Hamrin, Robert, *Making It In America*, (New York: Simon and Schuster), 1995, p. 221.

8. *Connection Technology*, November 1990, p. 16.

9. Jasinowski, p. 222.

10. *Ibid.*

11. Leonard Hill, interviewed by author, February 11, 1997. Transcript, p. 13.

12. McKeefry, Hailey Lynne, "Connector Makers Jump on the ISO– Certification Train," *Electronic Buyers' News*, Feb. 15, 1993, p. E16–17.

13. AMP 1995 Annual Report, p. 1.

14. Henry Line, interviewed by author, February 10, 1997. Transcript, p. 15.

15. AMP 1995 Annual Report, p. 1.

16. *Design News*, Nov. 23, 1992, p. 202.

17. Warner, Mary, "Kodak Tops AMP for the Baldridge," *Patriot– News*, Oct. 19, 1993, p. B3.

18. AMP 1993 Annual Report, p. 9.

19. James Marley, interviewed by Sel Friedlander, February 4, 1997. Transcript, pp. 34-35.

20. Levy, Corrine Bernstein, "Joint Ventures: A New Trend?" *Electronic Buyers' News*, Feb. 12, 1990.

21. Jorgensen, Barbara, "AMP Diversifies to Continue Growing," *Electronic Business Buyer*, October 1993.

22. Gupta, Udayan, "Strategic Alliances Hold Key To BroadBand's Financing," *The Wall Street Journal*, June 16, 1993: B2.

23. Norman, Diane, "AMP Accenting Systems Approach," *Electronic Buyers' News*, Sept. 7, 1992.

24. AMP 1992 Annual Report, p. 17.

25. Marley interview, p. 13.
26. *Ibid.*
27. AMP 1995 Annual Report, p. 2.
28. David Crockett, interviewed by Sel Friedlander, October 9, 1996. Transcript, page 14.
29. AMP 1990 Annual Report; and "Growing Internationally," *Electronic Business*, September 1991.
30. Jay L. Seitchik, interviewed by Jon VanZile, September 16, 1997.
31. McClenahen, John S., "Global Grasp," *Industry Week*, May 1993.

Chapter Ten

1. James Marley, interviewed by Sel Friedlander, December 19, 1988. Transcript, p. 4.
2. Robert Ripp, interviewed by author, February 12, 1997. Transcript, page 10.
3. Bill Oakland, interviewed by Jon VanZile, August 7, 1997.
4. Levine, Bernard, "What They're Saying," *Electronic News*, Oct. 5, 1992.
5. Warner, Mary, "AMP's Next Leader Reflects Sales Trend," *Patriot–News*, Oct. 4, 1992, p. F2.
6. Levine, Bernard, "What They're Saying," *Electronic News*, Oct. 5, 1992.
7. *Ibid.*
8. James Marley, interviewed by author, February 10, 1997. Transcript, p. 10.
9. Bill Urkiel, interviewed by Jon VanZile, August 4, 1997.

10. Bill Hudson, interviewed by Jon VanZile, August 4, 1997.
11. Bill Hudson, interviewed by author, July 9, 1997.
12. Joseph Overbaugh, interviewed by author, February 11, 1997. Transcript, p. 9.
13. Nazario Proietto, interviewed by Sel Friedlander, February 29, 1997. Transcript, p. 18.
14. Ted Dalrymple, interviewed by Sel Friedlander, November 1, 1996. Transcript, p. 23.
15. Dalrymple interview, p. 24.
16. Ron Vance, interviewed by author, February 12, 1997. Transcript, p. 11.
17. Howard Peiffer, interviewed by the author, February 10, 1997. Transcript, p. 13.
18. Linn Lightner, interviewed by author, February 11, 1997. Transcript, p. 11.
19. Phillipe Lemaitre, interviewed by Jon VanZile, August 4, 1997.
20. McCormick, Joel, "Connector Makers Buffeted By Shifting Market Factors," *Electronic Business*, Nov. 12, 1990, p. 111.
21. Xiaoge, Xiong, "U.S. Electronic Firms in China Attempt to Return to Normal," *Electronic Business*, Feb. 5, 1990, pp. 55–56.
22. "AMP in Joint Venture with Chinese Company," *Electronic Buyers' News*, March 23, 1992.
23. *Electronic Business Asia*, September 1991.

24. Herb Cole, interviewed by Sel Friedlander, June 12, 1996. Transcript, p. 22.
25. J.C. Tan, interviewed by Sel Freidlander, April 9, 1997. Transcript, p. 2.
26. David Toser, interviewed by Sel Friedlander, October 9, 1996. Transcript, page 6.
27. Charles Goonrey, interviewed by author, February 11, 1997. Transcript, p. 10.
28. Juergen Gromer, interviewed by Sel Friedlander, October 15, 1996. Transcript, p. 7.
29. Pete Glaser, interviewed by Sel Friedlander, October 14, 1996. Transcript, p. 2.
30. "AMP Plans Hungarian Manufacturing Plant," *Electronic Buyers' News*, Dec. 21, 1992.
31. AMP 1993 Annual Report, and AMP 1995 Annual Report.
32. Rudy Eckardt, interviewed by Sel Friedlander, October 14, 1996. Transcript, page 25.
33. Hal McInnes, interviewed by Sel Frieldander, May 2, 1996. Transcript, p. 10.
34. John Gurski, interviewed by author, February 10, 1997. Transcript, p. 12.
35. McClenahen, John S., *Industry Week*, 1993.
36. Robert Suares, interviewed by Sel Friedlander, October 17, 1996. Transcript, p. 6.
37. Franz Gall, interviewed by Sel Friedlander, Octber 16, 1996. Transcript, p. 9.
38. Harry Kennis, interviewed by Sel Friedlander, October 16, 1996. Transcript, p. 6.

39. AMP 1993 Annual Report, p. 1.

40. Warner, Mary, "Smart American Home to Become Part of AMP," *Patriot–News*, Dec. 11, 1993, A8.

41. Levine, Bernard, "The Package," *Electronic News*, Dec. 12, 1994.

42. DeKok, David, "AMP to Unveil Restructuring Plan Today," *Patriot-News*, Jan. 8, 1997, p. B5.

43. *International Directory of Company Histories*, ed. Tina Grant, p. 27.

44. "The Microwave Monitor," a 35th anniversary AMP report p. 8.

45. Richard Clark, interviewed by Jon Rounds, Feb. 4, 1997.

46. Byrne, Harlan S., "Well Connected," *Barron's*, April 24, 1995.

47. Norman, Diane, "AMP Set to Fold Subsidiary," *Electronic Buyers' News*, Aug. 8, 1994.

48. Norman, Diane, "AMP Backs Ailing Unit" *Electronic Buyers' News*, Aug. 10, 1992.

49. *Ibid.*

50. Norman, "AMP Set to Fold Subsidiary."

51. DeKok, David, "AMP to Shut Adams Site," *Patriot–News*, January 9, 1997, p. A8.

52. Richard Skaare, interviewed by author, February 10, 1997. Transcript, p. 16.

53. Robert Ripp, interviewed by Jon VanZile, August 13, 1997.

54. Bill Hudson, interviewed by author, July 9, 1997.

55. Leonard Hill, interviewed by author, July 10, 1997.

56. AMP 1996 Annual Report, p. 12.

57. AMP Annual Reports, 1990 through 1995.

58. DeKok, David, "AMP Posts Fourth–Quarter Loss," *Patriot–News*, Jan. 23, 1997, p. B1.

59. *Ibid.*

60. Oakland, interview by the author, p. 30.

61. AMP 1995 Annual Report.

62. *Ibid.*

63. Bill Oakland, interviewed by Jon VanZile, August 11, 1997.

64. Hudson, interviewed by the author, p. 32.

Chapter Ten Sidebar

1. Marshall Holcombe, interviewed by Sel Friedlander. Transcript, p. 3.

2. Hal McInnes, interviewed by Sel Frieldander, May 2, 1996. Transcript, p. 19.

3. Hal McInnes, interviewed by Jon VanZile, June 11, 1997.

4. Bill Hudson, interviewed by Jon VanZile, August 4, 1997.

INDEX